I0088749

# UNREAD
## My Journey to the Bible:
### *A Redemption Story*

## Michael Brannon

LUCIDBOOKS

**UNREAD: My Journey to the Bible: A Redemption Story**
Copyright © 2025 by Michael Brannon

Published by Lucid Books in Houston, TX
www.LucidBooks.com

All rights reserved. No part of this publication may be reproduced, stored in a retrieval system, or transmitted in any form by any means, electronic, mechanical, photocopy, recording, or otherwise, without the prior permission of the publisher, except as provided for by USA copyright law.

Unless otherwise indicated, scripture quotations are taken from the NIV® Holy Bible, New International Version®, Copyright ©1973, 1978, 1984, 2011 by Biblica, Inc.™ Used by permission of Zondervan. All rights reserved worldwide. www.zondervan.com The "NIV" and "New International Version" are trademarks registered in the United States Patent and Trademark Office by Biblica, Inc.™

ISBN: 978-1-63296-897-5 (paperback)
ISBN: 978-1-63296-898-2 (hardback)
eISBN: 978-1-63296-899-9

Special Sales: Most Lucid Books titles are available in special quantity discounts. Custom imprinting or excerpting can also be done to fit special needs. Contact Lucid Books at Info@LucidBooks.com

To the One who truly wrote this book:
I am not the author—just the one He chose to hold the pen.
All glory to God, the Creator, the Voice,
the Author of every word.

And to my wife and daughters:
Thank you for being the story of my life.
You are the pages I cherish most.

To my sons-in-law:
Thank you for loving my girls well and
for walking this road of faith alongside them.

And to my grandchildren:
You are the new chapter God is writing,
full of promise, purpose, and wonder.
May you always know how deeply you are loved.

# TABLE OF CONTENTS

# FOREWORD

One of the greatest joys in any ministry career is watching God get a hold of people and change them into someone they never thought they could or would be. The Lord has a lot of resources at His disposal to use in seen and unseen ways to unlock His plan and purpose for a life. He uses people, churches, life situations, and the Holy Spirit to shape a person's spiritual journey. This book is about an untapped, under-utilized resource that is available to almost everyone—a resource that changed the author in a profound way.

I have had the privilege of knowing Mike Brannon as his pastor and friend for about three years. One thing that impressed me about Mike from the start of our relationship is that he did not have the typical new retiree mindset. He wanted to continue growing and serving God in a deeper, better way. *Unread: My Journey to the Bible* is a chronicle of that journey. I have watched God deepen and better Mike, and both of us believe that is possible for anyone who reads this book.

I consistently encourage people to resist trying to be someone else in their service to the Lord. Each of us have a unique voice, and God speaks to us and through us in exceptional ways if we allow ourselves to be a channel for Him. Mike's voice is truly special. His book is humorous, poignant, self-deprecating, powerful, insightful, and moving. I seldom read a book that is impossible to put down and moves me to tears. This book has made me late for appointments and delayed my sermon preparation for the week.

Mike interweaves personal narratives with illustrative biblical teaching to great effect. He has written a book that will speak to the newest of Christians as well as people who have been going to church for decades. I plan to give a copy of this book to each of the new Christians at our church.

I highly encourage you to read this book with a highlighter and a box of tissues. Prepare to be changed!

**Dr. Sid Tiller,**
Senior Minister
Northside Christian Church
Warrensburg, Missouri

# SPECIAL THANKS

To my pastor and friend, **Sid Tiller**—thank you for letting me bounce ideas off you and for walking with me through the details of this book. When I grow up, I want to be just like you.

To my brother, **Larry**—thank you for your steady support throughout this project. Your prayers and encouragement carried me across the finish line.

# INTRODUCTION

*UNREAD: When the Bible stays closed . . . so does your heart.*

I'm not even sure books have introductions anymore. Do people still read those? Did they ever? If you're skimming this with a half cup of lukewarm coffee thinking, "I'll give him one paragraph." Well, thanks for that. And also, you should know that I'm not an author.

I never wanted to write a book. I don't even like reading books. If there were a movie version of the Bible, I would've watched that instead. (Wait—there is. I still didn't watch it.) So why am I writing this? Why now?

Because I made a promise. After a certain . . . let's call it life-altering event (we'll get there), I told God I would stop saying no and start saying yes to whatever He asked of me. He took me seriously.

This book is part of that yes. But saying yes meant more than just typing words. It meant ripping off the mask. It meant revisiting parts of my story I've spent a lifetime avoiding—fears I had buried, lies I had believed, and wounds I had kept hidden under a pretty decent smile. Writing this meant I had to open the vault. And let me tell you, that vault wasn't just dusty. It was fortified with shame, guarded by insecurity, and stacked wall-to-wall with stories I never wanted to tell anyone.

But I'm telling my stories now—not because I want sympathy and not because I have it all figured out. I'm telling them because reading the Bible changed my life sooner than I ever expected. Not because I read it like a scholar (I didn't). Not because I understood every page (I didn't). But because for the first time in my life, I let God speak through His Word instead of just letting someone else talk about it.

This isn't a Bible study nor is it a theology book. It's the story of how God used the Bible to rewrite everything I believed about myself—and how He can do the same for you.

I'm not a theologian. I didn't go to seminary. I'm just a guy who avoided the Bible for most of his life because I thought I didn't need it. I had pastors, podcasts, small groups, and church signs with clever slogans. That should've covered it, right?

And the Old Testament? I thought that was just there to make Leviticus jokes and remind me why I like bacon. The New Testament? I figured if I read a couple of the Gospels and then skipped to Paul's greatest hits, I was good.

I had no idea how wrong I was. I hope that when you finish this book, you'll understand why. I hope that you will understand that the whole Bible—every chapter, every struggle, every unlikely hero, every uncomfortable truth—is for you. It was for me. But before we dive into any of that, I need you to know who's talking to you.

This story starts before I ever opened a Bible. It starts with the one I'd been handed—the story that was told about me before I ever learned to speak for myself. The story that shaped me. Haunted me. The one that whispered for decades, "You're broken. You're not enough. You never were."

I wish that were an exaggeration. It's not.

## The Story That Named Me

It wasn't just a story I heard—it was the only story I knew. And it was mine. My mom would tell it like it was a badge of survival: "When you were born, you didn't cry. It was so quiet. Too quiet. I kept asking the doctors, 'What's wrong with my baby?'"

She said it felt like forever. Then, finally, I cried. Relief, right? Not quite. The doctor pulled her aside. I had been born with the umbilical cord wrapped around my neck. I hadn't breathed for four minutes. Blue baby syndrome, they called it.

And then came the sentence that stayed: "There could be brain damage." He didn't sugarcoat it. He added, "He could be retarded." I know. That word stings now, and thank God, we've outgrown it. But back then? It wasn't just a diagnosis. It was a label. One that stuck with me like invisible ink you could never wash off.

My mom didn't mean to harm me. I believe that. Maybe retelling it helped her process the fear. Maybe it reminded her I was a miracle. Maybe it was her way of coping with the worst moment of her life.

But for me? That story followed me like a shadow. It wasn't a celebration. It felt like a warning: "There's something wrong with him." My story was told at family dinners. To teachers. To strangers. Even to the girls I brought home. At some point, the story stopped sounding like a miracle and started sounding like a disclaimer. Like I had a defect no one could prove, but everyone silently agreed on.

No one ever followed it up with, "They were wrong. You're fine." Not even my dad. Especially not my dad. If I struggled in school, the whisper was always the same: "Remember what they said when he was born." If I made a mistake, someone would say, "We were told this could happen." And that was not said with concern or out of love. It was just tossed out like an explanation—an excuse. It felt like a way to say, "We expected this."

Over time, that story got baked into my identity. It stopped being about me and became me. I wasn't a miracle. I was a mistake that somehow survived the delivery room . . . not someone saved. I was someone who had to prove they were worth saving.

## The Bible I Didn't Know I Needed

Here's the thing about stories like that: When no one gives you a better one, you believe the only one you've heard. And when you believe the wrong story, you spend your whole life trying to outlive the label. You perform. You pretend. You build a résumé of worth. You also become very good at timing jokes to dodge deeper conversations—like emotional ninjas with a Bible in our back pocket, just in case you need to blend in.

But eventually, the façade cracks. Because no matter how much applause you collect or approval you chase, you can't outrun a lie that's still alive inside you. You might hide it under success, charm, or even spiritual talk—but it waits in the quiet. And when the noise fades and the spotlight shifts, it's still there, whispering doubts you were never meant to carry.

That's where the Bible came in for me—not as a rule book or as a guilt trip. But the Bible was the first place I ever heard a better story about who I am. It didn't come all at once. It wasn't a lightning bolt. But the more I read, the more I realized something: God didn't see me the way I saw myself.

He wasn't asking me to prove anything. He was inviting me to receive something. Truth. Healing. Identity. Worth. So yeah—this is my story. The good, the broken, the funny, the scarred. It's not polished. But it's real. And maybe, just maybe, it sounds a little like your story.

Maybe you've been living under a label you didn't ask for. Maybe someone told you a story about who you are, and it stuck.

Maybe you've been walking through life trying to earn what was never meant to be earned: your worth.

If that's you . . . if your soul is tired from the performance, from the pretending, from the pressure of holding it all together, then take this journey with me. Let's discover the truth together. Let's open the Bible not as a checklist but as a lifeline. Let's find out who God says we are—and finally silence the lies that have haunted us far too long and replace them with the truth that sets us free. Because the story you've been told isn't the one God is writing.

That's exactly how a man named Gideon felt thousands of years ago. He was told he was weak, insignificant, and unworthy, and he believed every word of it. But God had a different story to tell. Let's look at Gideon's story and see what happens when God's truth collides with the lies we've carried far too long.

# Chapter 1:
# THE LIES WE BELIEVE

*God calls us by the name of who we can become, not who we believe we are—and His truth is stronger than any lie we've carried.*

## Gideon's Lie – The Story

Gideon believed a lie: I am weak. I am the least. I don't matter. That lie wasn't whispered just once; it echoed in every day of his life. His family was part of the weakest clan in the tribe of Manasseh, and Gideon considered himself the lowest in his father's house (Judges 6:15). He had grown up in a culture crushed by fear, watching the Midianites sweep in year after year to steal everything. Over time, Gideon's identity shrank until it fit perfectly into the story he'd been told: You're powerless. You're nothing.

So, when we first see him, he's not standing tall; he's hiding in a winepress, threshing wheat in secret to avoid the raiders. He's surviving, not living. And if you've ever felt like you had to shrink yourself, hide your struggles, or pretend everything's fine just to get through the day, you know exactly what that feels like.

Then, into Gideon's small, fearful world, the angel of the Lord appeared and declared words that made no sense in light of Gideon's story: "*The Lord is with you, mighty warrior*" (Judges 6:12). Can you imagine Gideon's reaction? Mighty warrior? The man crouched in a pit, who probably hadn't felt brave a single day in his life? He must have thought God had the wrong address.

Gideon's response revealed how deeply the lie had taken root: "*Pardon me, my Lord . . . but if the Lord is with us, why has all this happened to us? Where are all his wonders . . . ? But now the Lord has abandoned us*" (Judges 6:13).

He questioned God's goodness, feeling forgotten and defeated. God didn't scold him for his doubts. He simply replied: "*Go in the strength you have and save Israel. . . . Am I not sending you*" (Judges 6:14)? But Gideon's old story still fought for control: "*Pardon me, my Lord . . . but how can I save Israel? . . . My clan is the weakest in Manasseh, and I am the least in my family*" (Judges 6:15).

And here comes the turning point—the truth powerful enough to rewrite any story: "*I will be with you, and you will strike down all the Midianites*" (Judges 6:16). Victory wouldn't come because Gideon suddenly became strong, but because God was with him.

Even so, Gideon needed reassurance. He asked for signs—first with fire consuming an offering, then twice with fleece and dew, and God patiently confirmed His promise every time. God wasn't offended by Gideon's fears; he met him in them.

When it was time for battle, Gideon gathered 32,000 men—finally something that looked like strength. But God had other plans: The army was too big. If Israel won with so many men, they would claim credit. So, God whittled the army down to just 300—an absurdly small number against an enemy described as thick as locusts (Judges 7:12).

These 300 men didn't carry swords; they carried trumpets, clay jars, and torches. At Gideon's signal, they smashed their jars, blew the trumpets, and shouted: "*A sword for the* Lord *and for Gideon*" (Judges 7:20)? God threw the Midianite camp into chaos, and the enemy turned on each other. Israel was freed not because Gideon had power, but because God's power was made perfect in Gideon's weakness.

This isn't just a story of one man overcoming fear; it's a turning point in which God revealed what happens when His truth collides with the lies, we've believed—rewriting not only Gideon's identity, but Israel's future. It's the moment a man who saw himself as the weakest became God's chosen warrior, showing us that our perceived limitations don't define us—God's calling does.

## What Can We Learn from Gideon's Story?

Gideon's story isn't just about a man hiding in fear—it's about a God who steps into that fear and calls us by a better name. When we feel weak, overlooked, or disqualified, Gideon's journey reminds us that we are not defined by our doubts or past failures but by what God sees in us. While Gideon hid in a winepress, believing he was the least and the last, God called him "*mighty warrior.*" That title wasn't based on what Gideon had done; it was based on what God was about to do through him.

We all have places we hide—buried under insecurity, past wounds, or fear of failure. But Gideon's story shows us that:

- God sees what we can't. He sees potential where we see problems.
- God renames us with purpose. He speaks identity over us before we ever prove ourselves.
- God's presence is our power. Gideon wasn't told to believe in himself; he was told to believe God would be with him.
- God's truth rewrites the lies. What we've believed for years can be overturned by one word from the One who knows us best.

Gideon's call wasn't an isolated moment; it was part of God's bigger story of redemption. Israel had turned away from God and was suffering under Midianite rule, yet God, rich in mercy, raised up a deliverer. Not a warrior, but a fearful man from the weakest tribe. His victory, accomplished with just 300 men, wasn't a celebration of human strength; it was a declaration of divine power. It pointed to the way God always works, which is through weakness, so that no one can boast (2 Corinthians 12:9). Just as Gideon delivered Israel, Jesus would come as the ultimate Deliverer—humble, unexpected, and unstoppable.

Gideon's story is a thread in God's rescue plan—a reminder that God sees us, calls us out of hiding, and invites us into His mission. When we believe Him, even with trembling hands, we step into the purpose we were made for. So, if you've ever felt stuck, silenced, or small, remember Gideon: If God could use a frightened man in a winepress to rescue a nation, He can certainly use you to change the world around you.

## Mary Magdalene – The Story

*Jesus doesn't flinch at your darkest moments; He runs toward them to call you by name and make you new.*

Mary Magdalene knew what it was like to be defined by darkness. She wasn't just struggling or making mistakes; she was possessed by seven demons (Luke 8:2). Can you imagine the terror? The loss of control? The looks of disgust on people's faces as they crossed the street to avoid her? She wasn't Mary the friend, Mary the daughter, or Mary the dreamer—she was Mary the Madwoman, Mary the Lost Cause.

Every whisper about her, every sidelong glance, every door slammed in her face repeated the same lie: You're too far gone. You're beyond help. You are nothing but a burden.

But then Jesus came. He didn't recoil from her brokenness or shame. He saw the real Mary beneath the torment—the woman he created, loved, and came to rescue. With a word, He shattered the grip of darkness and silenced the lies that had haunted her for years. For the first time, Mary was free. And she knew it wasn't because of her strength or worthiness, but because of His unstoppable love.

From that day on, Mary followed Jesus with everything she had. She became one of His most devoted supporters, traveling with Him and the disciples, giving out of her resources to help share His message (Luke 8:1–3).

When the world's darkness closed in on Jesus at the cross, Mary didn't run. She stood there, heartbroken but loyal, as her Savior died. When others hid in fear, she went to the tomb at dawn, still searching for the One who gave her hope when she had none. And in the garden of the empty tomb, through her tears, she heard the voice she knew better than any other: "*Mary*" (John 20:16).

In that single word, Jesus did what only He can do: He called her by name, restored her identity, and gave her a mission that would change everything. Mary, once a prisoner of darkness, became the first witness of the resurrection, entrusted with the greatest news the world has ever known.

## What Can We Learn from Mary's Story?

Mary Magdalene's life proves that no one is too far gone for Jesus. Once tormented by seven demons, she was seen by others as broken, but Jesus saw someone worth saving, healing, and sending.

She didn't just receive freedom; she received a new identity. While others fled, Mary stayed near—even at the cross and the tomb. Because of her faithfulness, she became the first witness of the resurrection, the first to hear the risen Jesus speak. And He called her by name.

Her story speaks to anyone who's felt too broken, too sinful, or forgotten. Jesus didn't just forgive Mary—He commissioned her. Her life reminds us that Jesus meets us in our mess, rewrites our story, and sends us out to share His story.

In a world that tried to silence her, Jesus amplified Mary's voice. And He's still doing the same today—calling names, rewriting stories, and using the unlikely person to change the world.

# Chapter 2:
# WHY WE DON'T READ
# THE BIBLE

*We come up with every possible reason not to read the Bible—
too tired, too busy, too broken—and somehow, God keeps
showing up between the lines anyway, waiting with truth we
didn't know we needed and grace we never earned.*

Since you're reading this book, chances are you've already thought about reading the Bible—or felt bad about not reading it more. Maybe you've even tried once or twice. You got a nice leather-bound version of the Bible, opened it with noble intentions, started reading somewhere in the Old Testament, and thought, "Wait, what is happening? Why are we measuring tent poles and sacrificing goats?"

So, you closed it. Gently. And put it back on the shelf like it was radioactive.

You're not alone. Reading the Bible can feel like deciding to run a marathon when you've barely made it around the block. You know it's good for you. You know, people talk about how life-changing it is. But getting started feels awkward, and sticking with it feels even harder.

Sometimes, the Bible ends up on the same shelf—physically and emotionally—as the treadmill we bought with good intentions, the gym membership we're "totally going to use," or the guitar we were going to learn to play. The Word of God becomes the most important thing we keep saying we'll get around to. Someday.

And just like those other things . . . we feel a little guilty every time we walk past it. But let me tell you something: That guilt doesn't come from God. God isn't holding a cosmic clipboard, checking off boxes on your Bible reading habits. He's not sighing in disappointment or throwing up His hands like, well, I guess they're not getting it today. That's not His heart. He's not frustrated with your lack of discipline; He's longing for your attention. He wants to meet you in His Word—not to grade you, but to grow you.

This book isn't here to make you feel bad about not reading your Bible. It's here to help you understand why you haven't read your Bible and why it matters so much that you start.

## Why Don't We Read the Bible?

Let's be real: The Bible can be intimidating. It's big. It's old. It has names you can't pronounce. It references places you've never been and customs that feel . . . well, very foreign. Reading it without help can feel like watching a twelve-hour documentary on something you don't understand, with no subtitles and no coffee.

And yet, it's also the most powerful, personal, and transformative book ever written. It's the one book that's alive—a book that reads you while you read it. That's not just poetic. It's real. The Bible doesn't just tell you what happened; it tells you what's happening in you. As you read, it gently uncovers what you've been avoiding, what needs healing, and what God is trying to grow in you.

Jeremiah 23:29 says, "*Is not my word like fire," declares the Lord, "and like a hammer that breaks a rock in pieces?*" It burns away lies. It breaks through walls. While you think you're studying the Word, it's studying you, shaping you from the inside out.

But most of us don't experience it that way. We hesitate. We delay. We stay distant. We're like someone who says they want to get in shape but never wants to sweat. Or someone who buys a ticket to a concert but stays outside the venue because they have a fear of crowds.

And here's the thing: We're not bad people for struggling with this. We're just human—busy, tired, distracted, and overstimulated humans. We avoid the Bible because we think it's going to confront us, and it will. But what we forget is: It also invites us. It invites us:

- Into grace—the kind that silences shame and reminds us we're loved as we are.
- Into healing—deep, honest healing that reaches places we didn't know were broken.
- Into joy—not just happiness when life goes right, but joy that holds steady when it doesn't.
- Into wisdom—the kind that sees with God's eyes, not just our own.
- And into peace—real peace. The kind Jesus gives, not the kind the world pretends to offer.

## Avoiding the Bible

I didn't grow up in church. I didn't have a Bible by my bed or anyone praying over me at night. Nobody was quoting Scripture over pancakes or pointing me to God when life got confusing. Looking back, I think I just assumed that kind of closeness with God was for other people—for families who had it together, who knew what love and safety were supposed to feel like.

To me, God felt distant. Not angry—just far away. Like a name you hear often but never get to say for yourself—like, He belonged to someone else's story, not mine.

As a teen, someone introduced me to Jesus, and I believed. I accepted Him as my Savior. But I'll be honest: I didn't open the Bible right away. Not regularly. Not deeply. I told myself I would. I even carried one to church. But my real relationship with Scripture was more like a handshake than a conversation. I nodded at it. I respected it. But I didn't know it.

And because I didn't know God's Word, I didn't know God. Not in a way that changed me. Not in a way that healed the deep parts of me—the shame, the fear, the control, the questions I was too afraid to ask out loud. I was a Christian. But I was a Christian who didn't read the Bible. And it showed.

In time, I started to hear about this God who loved me. A God who forgives, who heals, who invites you into peace. And I wanted that. Desperately. But then I'd go home and find that nothing had changed. There was the same dysfunction, the same silence, and the same weight.

My emotions were all over the place. I'd pray, hoping to hear something back, but all I got was quiet. I'd go to church and feel a flicker of hope, but by the time I got back to my real life, the feeling would fade. I believed God could bring peace—I just didn't understand how to follow the path to it while everything around me felt so unstable. Looking back, I wasn't a bad person. I was just unrooted, and unrooted trees don't stand up well in storms.

## What This Book Will Do

This book is here to help you get rooted. Not just in religion. Not in routines. But in the living, breathing Word of God.

We're going to walk through some hard truths and ask uncomfortable questions. We're going to laugh. (Trust me—we need to.) We're going to hit pause on shame and hit play on growth. And we're going to learn how to stop making excuses and start walking in the kind of faith that changes everything.

We'll talk through the ten biggest reasons we avoid the Bible. (You've probably used at least seven.) We'll counter each one with truth and encouragement. Then we'll look at ten better reasons to read the Bible—and understand how your life begins to shift when you do.

Along the way, I'll share my story—not because it's special, but because it's real. I wandered for years. I wanted the blessing of salvation without the discomfort of surrender. But at some point, I had to choose: Either I would stay in control and keep struggling, or I would finally open the Bible and let God show me who He is. Spoiler: I opened it. And I wish I had done so sooner.

Here's how *Unread: My Journey to the Bible:A Redemption Story* works: In each chapter, I'll tell you a piece of my story—raw, honest, and probably messier than you'd expect from someone writing a book about faith. Then, in the next section, we'll look at God's story. We'll open Scripture to see how the Bible speaks directly to the same struggles, fears, or questions I faced. We'll meet people who messed up, ran away, tried to hide, doubted, or found redemption—and see how God met them in every moment.

Because the Bible isn't just an ancient book; it's God's voice still speaking today. "*For the word of God is alive and active. Sharper than any double-edged sword*" (Hebrews 4:12). When we read His Word alongside our own stories, we start to see His fingerprints on every chapter of our lives.

So come along for the ride. We'll laugh, we'll wrestle with big questions, and together we'll discover a God who isn't afraid of our mess—and who never stops inviting us closer.

## Ten Real Reasons (Let's Be Honest—Excuses) Why We Don't Read the Bible

1. **It's confusing.** Let's not sugarcoat this. You open the Old Testament, and suddenly you're wading through instructions for building a tent you're never going to pitch and names that sound like someone sneezed while typing. You came for encouragement and ended up in a scroll-length episode of what sounds like "This Old Tabernacle."

   Here's what I wish someone had told me earlier: The Bible isn't a single book—it's a library. Sixty-six books, written over 1,500 years, in three languages, across multiple continents, by poets, fishermen, kings, prophets, and a tentmaker or two. Of course, it feels confusing at first; it was written for you, but not originally to you. That's why we need guidance, context, and patience.

   But confusing doesn't mean inaccessible. We watch YouTube videos to fix our washing machines. We Google symptoms like we're studying for med school. The same curiosity that drives us to learn anything else can help us uncover the treasure in God's Word. God promises it won't be a waste of time: "*It* [my Word] *will not return to me empty, but will accomplish what I desire*" (Isaiah 55:11). Don't fear the confusion. Start with curiosity.

2. **I don't have time.** Not enough time. The holy grail of excuses. And listen, I've used it too. I've got a full-time job. I've raised kids. I've lived through seasons of stress, ministry,

deadlines, and trying to be everything for everyone. I get it. But let's get brutally honest for a second: We make time for what matters to us.

We scroll our phones for hours. We binge-watch shows we won't even remember next year. We research fantasy football stats, scroll through home DIY ideas, or read comment sections (which, let's admit, are soul-draining rabbit holes). The question isn't, "Do I have time?" It's "What am I trading my time for?"

If the Bible is what it says it is—alive, powerful, God-breathed, then how can we afford not to make time for it?

*Fix these words of mine in your hearts and minds . . . .*
*Teach them to your children, talking about them when*
*you sit at home and when you walk along the road,*
*when you lie down and when you get up.*
　　　　　　　　　　　　　—Deuteronomy 11:18–19

This isn't about finding a perfect hour of silence. It's about inviting God's Word into your normal, busy, imperfect life.

3. **It feels boring.** Somewhere between the genealogy of Numbers and the laws in Leviticus, we start questioning our life choices. We were looking for divine inspiration and found ourselves reading about mildew inspections and animal sacrifices. But here's the thing: The Bible isn't boring—we've just approached it like a textbook instead of a story.

The Bible contains epic battles, betrayal, scandal, redemption, angels, floods, resurrections, talking animals, and a Savior who defeats death. If that's boring, we might need to check our pulse.

Still, I get it. If we try to read the Bible like we're checking off a to-do list, it feels boring. But when we start reading the Bible like it's a conversation and when we come asking God what he wants to show us today, everything changes.

4. **It makes me feel guilty.** This one hits close to home. I used to avoid the Bible because I was afraid of what it would show me. I didn't want to see my sin, my pride, my selfishness, and my wounds. I thought Scripture was just there to expose all the ways I'd failed. And, of course, some days, it did show me things I didn't want to see.

But over time, I realized something: Conviction isn't condemnation. God doesn't show us our brokenness to shame us; He shows it so He can heal us. As the Apostle Paul says in Romans 8:1: "*There is now no condemnation for those who are in Christ Jesus.*"

The Bible is a mirror, not a magnifying glass. It reflects the truth, not to destroy us, but to invite us to something better.

5. **I've already heard it at church.** Church is great. So is preaching. But relying solely on Sunday sermons to feed your spirit is like surviving on one meal a week and wondering why you're starving by Tuesday. God wants to speak to you, not just through your pastor, but through the pages of His Word.

Besides, have you ever rewatched a movie and caught something new the second time? Or the fifth? That's how Scripture works. It's layered, alive. You could read the same verse 100 times and get something fresh on the 101st reading. That's why, as you reading through this book, you may see Scriptures repeated.

Still with me? Good. Because we're only halfway through, and chances are . . . we haven't hit your favorite excuse yet.

6. **I don't know where to start.** Here's a secret: You don't have to start at the beginning.

    The Bible isn't like a novel. You don't have to begin in Genesis and go straight through to Revelation (though you can!). Start with the Gospels—Matthew, Mark, Luke, and John. Read about Jesus. Get to know Him. Or read Psalms when you're anxious, Proverbs when you need wisdom, or Ephesians when you feel stuck. There's no wrong place to start—only wrong reasons not to.

7. **It's irrelevant to modern life.** The Bible doesn't mention Instagram or streaming or email stress or road rage. But it does talk about anxiety, identity, betrayal, pride, sex, money, grief, purpose, power, leadership, parenting, injustice, loneliness, hope, suffering, and forgiveness. Tell me that's not relevant.

    The faces and technology may have changed, but the human heart hasn't. The Word speaks to our real lives—right now, in real time.

8. **It's hard to understand.** Yes. Some passages are hard to understand as they contain symbolism or address culture and prophecy. But hard doesn't mean impossible. Start by using a Bible translation that speaks clearly to you (we'll talk about that later). Get a study Bible. Find a guide. Ask questions. You're not dumb. You're just learning something deep and eternal. Give yourself grace. God does. And don't forget that you've got the Holy Spirit—your built-in translator.

9.  **I feel disconnected from God.** Ironically, this is often why we avoid the Bible—and the very reason we need it most. When you feel distant from God, that is not the time to run from His Word—it's the time to run to it.

    Feeling disconnected doesn't mean God has moved. Sometimes, it means we've stopped listening. But His Word is always there. Always speaking. Always waiting.

10. **I'm afraid it might change me.** This is the one most of us never say out loud. We know the Bible might mess with our lives. It might tell us to let go of some stuff, to forgive someone, to change a behavior, or to surrender something we like holding onto. And honestly, that can be terrifying.

    But here's the truth: Change is what we're longing for. Deep down, we want transformation, but we're just scared of the cost. But the cost of staying stuck is so much higher.

## My Story – Why This Matters

I wasn't raised in a spiritual family. We didn't gather around the table to read devotionals. Nobody was quoting Jeremiah over breakfast. We weren't even lukewarm—we were just lost.

Faith wasn't hostile in our house. It was just . . . absent—like a light switch that no one ever thought to flip on. So, when I finally heard the message of Jesus as a teenager, and someone told me I could be saved, loved, and made new, I said yes. And I meant it.

I accepted Christ as my Savior. I truly believed He died for me. I wanted to go to heaven. I even wanted to live a better life here on earth. But what I didn't want—what I didn't even realize I needed—was to surrender. I didn't know that was part of the deal. I thought showing up was enough. I didn't understand that peace doesn't come without letting go.

I didn't want to give up control. I didn't want to let anyone—not even Jesus—rewrite my story. I had been trying to manage myself; even as a child, I was trying to write the narrative. I knew, or thought I knew, what I wanted people to see. So, for years, I lived in this weird spiritual no-man's land: saved but not surrendered. Forgiven, but still living like I had to earn everything. I went to church. I served. I smiled. I said the right words.

But I wasn't reading the Bible with any real consistency. Why? Because deep down, I knew that if I opened it, something in me would have to change. And I wasn't ready for that.

I was still trying to control the steering wheel, chart the course, and manage the outcome. I wanted Jesus in the passenger seat, not the driver's seat. And if I'm honest, I didn't want to read his Word because I didn't want to give him that much say in how I lived my life.

That's the thing about Scripture: It doesn't just inform; it transforms. And transformation is uncomfortable—especially when you've built your whole identity around performance, self-sufficiency, and the illusion of control.

## Savior versus Lord

There's a difference between saying, "Jesus saved me," and saying, "Jesus leads me." Most of us want a Savior. We want forgiveness. We want peace. We want the insurance policy for when life falls apart.

But Lordship? That's a whole different level. When Jesus is Lord, He doesn't just clean up our messes. He calls the shots. He sets the direction. He holds the map. And His Word becomes the compass for every single step. Jesus said, "*If anyone would come after me, he must deny himself and take up his cross daily and follow me*" (Luke 9:23). Daily. Not just on Sundays. Not just when it's convenient. Every. Single. Day. That's what I had to learn the hard way.

I spent over forty years calling myself a Christian while living like the CEO of my own life. Then God brought me to a breaking point where my carefully built plans collapsed, and I was finally forced to ask: What if the life I've been building isn't the one God had for me at all?

I wish I had opened the Bible sooner. I wish I had let his voice be louder than mine earlier. I would've saved myself a lot of heartache, regret, and confusion. But here's the beauty of grace: God didn't give up on me. He waited. He pursued. And when I finally picked up His Word and began to read it—not for knowledge, but for relationship, everything began to change.

## What I Want for You

The fact that you're reading this book tells me that something in you is already stirring. Maybe you're where I was—faithful in belief but hesitant to surrender. Maybe you've never opened a Bible and have no idea where to start. Or maybe you've been around Scripture your whole life but feel like it's grown cold, distant, or dull.

Wherever you are, this is your invitation. Not from me but from God. Take off the bib. Put on an apron. Don't just be fed—learn to feast. Dig into the Word and let it shape you. Don't just read it to check a box; read it because the Author knows you, loves you, and wants to walk with you.

This isn't a lecture. It's a conversation. This isn't a rule book. It's a rescue plan. This isn't a burden. It's a gift.

## Without God's Word, We Drift

We drift into old habits; into false identities; into anxiety, shame, distraction, and self-dependence. We start living on fumes. We rely on memory verses from childhood or sermons from last month to keep our hearts going. But that's not enough.

The Bible is like water to the soul. Without it, our spiritual life becomes stagnant, like a pond with no fresh flow. "Blessed is the one . . . whose delight is in the law of the Lord. . . . That person is like a tree planted by streams of water" (Psalm 1:1–3 paraphrased). Without the Word, we become dry, fragile, and easily shaken.

## When We Open the Bible

When we open the Bible with expectation—even with confusion or hesitation—we meet God in the pages. We discover who he is and who we are. We see the lies we've believed, the wounds he wants to heal, and the purpose he's placed in us since the beginning. We hear his voice. We gain wisdom. We learn peace. We stop chasing approval and start walking in identity.

Reading Scripture roots us, grows us, and transforms us. It doesn't always feel dramatic. Some days, it feels quiet. But over time, it changes us from the inside out.

## What You Find in This Book

This book is your invitation to start or restart a lifelong relationship with the Bible. I'm not inviting you to approach the Bible in a heavy, theological, academic way but in a real, clear, personal way. What I have in mind is an approach that makes you say, "I get it now. I want more."

We're going to unpack the real reasons we tend to avoid the Bible, some of which we discussed earlier. We'll dig into why we can't afford to ignore the Bible and what happens when we finally commit. You'll hear more of my story—and more of God's. We'll walk through key Old Testament moments and meet Jesus in the Gospels. We'll learn to interpret, apply, and trust what we read.

Most of all, we'll learn how to listen because before you can follow Jesus, you have to know His voice.

## A Final Word Before We Move On

There's no shame in how long it's taken you to open your Bible. There's only joy in the fact that you're about to do so. If you stick with what you learn here—if you dig in with humility and hunger—I promise you'll begin to see Scripture not as a burden but as your lifeline. You won't always feel it. You won't always understand it. But you will never regret reading it.

In this chapter, we've talked about the excuses we make for avoiding the Bible—those reasons we cling to for staying comfortable, staying distracted, or staying in control. But what does God's Word say about excuses?

That's where we go next. We're going to step into the story of Moses, who gave God every excuse he could think of when called to something bigger than himself. Then we'll meet Jesus's first disciple, who made no excuses at all when the call came.

So, let's open these pages together, see what Scripture says about our hesitations, and discover what happens when we finally drop our excuses and say yes to God.

# Chapter 3:
# NO WAITING

*When God calls, don't wait: Obedience today opens doors tomorrow.*

## Moses and the Bush – The Story

Moses had settled into a life of obscurity in the wilderness. Decades had passed since he fled Egypt in fear, after killing an Egyptian in a failed attempt to deliver his people. The man who once dreamed of greatness was now a shepherd for his father-in-law's flocks—a humbling job for someone raised in Pharaoh's palace. Day after day, he guided sheep through dry, rugged hills, likely wondering if God had forgotten him or if his past failures had disqualified him forever.

But one day, while tending the sheep near Horeb, the mountain of God, Moses noticed something astonishing: a bush that blazed with fire yet was not consumed. Fire was common in the wilderness, but this fire was different—alive, unquenchable, holy. Intrigued, Moses stepped closer, drawn by curiosity and a sense of awe.

That's when everything changed. From within the flames, a voice called out, "*Moses! Moses*" (Exodus 3:4)! The God of Abraham, Isaac, and Jacob was speaking. Moses answered with a trembling, "*Here I am*," (Exodus 3:4), but God warned him not to come any closer. "*Take off your sandals, for the place where you are standing is holy ground*" (Exodus 3:5). The air must have felt heavy with the weight of God's presence. Moses hid his face, afraid to look at God, overwhelmed by the realization that he stood before the Lord of the universe.

God spoke with burning compassion: "*I have indeed seen the misery of my people in Egypt. I have heard them crying. . . . I am concerned about their suffering. So, I have come down to rescue them*" (Exodus 3:7–8). God wasn't indifferent; He had seen every tear, every crack of the whip, and every hopeless sigh. His heart broke for his people, and he was determined to save them.

But then God's words took a shocking turn: "*So now, go. I am sending you to Pharaoh to bring my people the Israelites out of Egypt*" (Exodus 3:10). Moses's heart must have pounded. Go back to Egypt? Confront the most powerful ruler on earth? Lead a nation out of bondage? His mind must have flashed with memories of his crime, his failure, his fears.

His first instinct was to doubt himself: "*Who am I that I should go*" (Exodus 3:11)? He was filled with shame, unworthiness, and fear. But God didn't respond with a pep talk; he offered his presence: "*I will be with you*" (Exodus 3:12). God's promise wasn't that Moses was strong enough, but that he would go with Moses.

Still, Moses scrambled for excuses: What if they ask who sent me? What if they don't believe me? Then God revealed his eternal name: "*I AM WHO I AM*" (Exodus 3:14); this name declares God's unchanging nature and sovereign authority. Then he gave Moses signs: a staff that turned into a snake, a hand that became leprous and was healed, and the promise of turning the Nile's water into blood. Each sign declared God's power over creation, disease, and the gods of Egypt.

But Moses wasn't done hesitating. His old wounds surfaced: "*Pardon your servant, Lord. I have never been eloquent. . . . I am slow of speech and tongue*" (Exodus 4:10). Perhaps he stammered as he said it, his insecurity laid bare. God's response was both tender and powerful: "*Who gave human beings their mouths? . . . Now go; I will help you speak and will teach you what to say*" (Exodus 4:11–12).

Yet Moses still pleaded, "*Please send someone else*" (Exodus 4:13). Even face to face with God, he felt trapped by fear. God's patience wore thin, but His plan never wavered. He appointed Aaron, Moses's brother, to help speak, but Moses would still carry the staff of God. God refused to let Moses's excuses derail His mission to save His people.

When Moses finally obeyed, he returned to Egypt with a staff in his hand and a fire in his soul. He confronted Pharaoh, called down plagues, split the Red Sea, and led Israel to freedom. The man who once ran away became the man who led millions out of slavery—not because he was fearless, but because God's power was greater than his excuses.

## What Can We Learn from Moses's Story?

God doesn't call the qualified; He qualifies the called. When Moses stood before the burning bush full of fear, shame, and excuses, God didn't give him a motivational speech; He gave him a promise: "*I will be with you*" (Exodus 3:12).

God chose a man who stuttered, doubted, and ran from his past to lead a nation out of slavery—not because of his ability, but to display God's power through human weakness. Our fears and failures don't disqualify us; they often become the very places where God's grace shines brightest.

Throughout Scripture, we see this same truth: Peter the doubter became the rock, Gideon the coward became a warrior, and Esther the orphan became a queen who saved her people. God isn't waiting for us to have it all together; He's simply waiting for our yes.

Moses's call wasn't just personal; it was part of God's bigger rescue plan. His obedience led to the exodus, the giving of the law, and the birth of Israel as a nation. It fulfilled God's promises to Abraham and pointed forward to a greater Deliverer—Jesus Christ—who would lead all people out of spiritual bondage.

The burning bush revealed a God who sees, hears, and acts to rescue. Moses's story is a powerful reminder that God uses imperfect people to accomplish His perfect will and that His promises, once given, never fail. Through Moses, we see the heart of a God who relentlessly pursues His people and invites them into a mission far bigger than themselves.

## Jesus Calls His First Disciple – The Story

*When Jesus says, "Follow me," the ordinary becomes extraordinary—and the life you know gives way to the purpose you were made for.*

The Sea of Galilee sparkled under the morning sun as Simon Peter and his brother Andrew sat slumped in their boat, exhausted from a night of fishing gone horribly wrong. They had cast their nets again and again, fighting frustration and fatigue under a sky full of stars, but the waters yielded nothing. Their hands were raw; their clothes smelled of stale water and sweat; and their hearts sagged under the weight of another day of empty nets. Fishing wasn't just their job; it was their survival, and they were coming up short.

Nearby, the shoreline was alive with people pressing toward a man teaching with a voice that carried authority and compassion. This was Jesus, already known for his astonishing words and miraculous healings. But as the crowd surged around him, they nearly shoved him into the water. Glancing up, Jesus stepped toward Simon's empty boat and asked him for help: "*Put out a little from shore*" (Luke 5:3). Simon, tired and probably annoyed, agreed. After all, what harm could it do?

Sitting in Simon's boat, Jesus taught the crowds while Simon repaired his torn nets—nets he believed wouldn't see a single fish that day. When the teaching finished, Jesus turned to Simon with a request that must have sounded absurd: "*Put out into deep water, and let down the nets for a catch*" (Luke 5:4). Simon's voice likely cracked with weary sarcasm: "*Master, we've worked hard all night and haven't caught anything. But because you say so, I will let down the nets*" (Luke 5:5).

Everything in Peter's experience told him it was pointless: fish don't bite in the heat of the day. But he obeyed. And suddenly, the impossible happened. The nets bulged and strained. Fish swirled and thrashed, flashing silver in the sun. Simon and Andrew pulled desperately, calling for help as the catch threatened to swamp their boat. James and John, the sons of Zebedee, raced over in their boat, their eyes wide as they grabbed the nets. Both boats groaned under the weight, nearly sinking under the bounty.

Simon's heart slammed in his chest. He knew fishing. He knew Galilee. This wasn't luck; this was a miracle, a sign of divine power. Overwhelmed, he fell among the flopping fish at Jesus's feet, eyes full of tears: "*Go away from me, Lord; I am a sinful man*" (Luke 5:8)! It was a confession born of awe and fear; Simon saw himself as unworthy to even stand in Jesus's presence.

But Jesus didn't move away. He smiled with the warmth of a Father and spoke words that changed everything: "*Don't be afraid;*

*from now on you will fish for people*" (Luke 5:10). His words cut through Peter's shame and invited him to a purpose bigger than he could imagine—one that would ripple across history.

On the shore, Peter, Andrew, James, and John faced a choice: Keep the biggest payday of their lives or walk away to follow a carpenter from Nazareth. They looked at the mountain of fish, the nets they'd always depended on, and then at Jesus, and chose Him. "*They pulled their boats up on shore, left everything and followed him*" (Luke 5:11). No hesitation. No going back.

## What Can We Learn from the First Disciples?

Jesus often calls us when we feel least ready—when we're tired, unqualified, or unsure. That's exactly how He called His first disciples—ordinary fishermen, weary from failure, invited into something extraordinary. Their response was immediate and radical; they dropped everything without hesitation.

Through their obedience, we see what true discipleship looks like: It means laying down what we rely on most and trusting Jesus to lead us somewhere better. The disciples' story challenges us, because unlike them, we often hesitate, clinging to comfort, control, or plans we made without God. But it's in saying yes without delay that we find the joy, purpose, and adventure we were created for. Following Jesus may not come with a detailed plan, but it always comes with deeper meaning and greater freedom.

The call of those first disciples wasn't just a personal moment; it was the beginning of a movement that would change the world. Jesus didn't choose the elite or powerful; He chose humble men willing to follow. Their yes launched the Church and fulfilled God's promise to bless all nations through Abraham's descendants (Genesis 12:3).

Their obedience turned the world upside down—not because they were perfect, but because they were willing. Their story reminds us that God still builds His kingdom through ordinary people who trust Him with everything. And just like them, we can't follow boldly if we don't know the One we're following. Scripture anchors us in His truth, fuels our faith, and teaches us what it means to walk with Jesus daily. With His Word in our hands, we can hear His call, stand firm in our faith, and step into the purpose for which we were made.

# Chapter 4:
# WHY WE NEED THE BIBLE

*We need the Bible not just to learn about God, but to hear Him speak into the places no one else sees. When we open it, He opens us—and that's when healing begins.*

### The Stranger We Say We're Following

Imagine this. Someone yells to you from across a crowded street, "Hey! Come follow me!" and without asking questions, without even knowing their name, you start trailing behind them. You follow them into alleys, through tunnels, into dark woods, over cliffs—and only after miles of walking do you finally whisper, "Uh . . . who are you?"

That's what many of us have done with Jesus. We said yes to salvation. We raised our hands, we walked down the aisle, we filled out the little card in church. But we never really got to know Him. And if I'm being honest, I didn't either—not for a long time.

## The Car Window Test

When I first met my wife, the woman I've now been married to for over forty-three years, I was just a young guy trying to figure things out. I didn't have much, certainly not a fancy car. In fact, the doors on my car didn't even open properly. So, every time we went somewhere, she had to crawl through the window like we were robbing a gas station. I half-expected her to yell, "Go! Go! Go!" every time we got in the car.

And not once—not once—did she complain. I remember watching her climb in, laughing to herself, acting like it was normal. And I thought, that's it. This is the girl. It wasn't just her sense of humor. It was her grace, her patience, her quiet strength, and her faith. It was the way she made everything feel lighter. I knew—even with my busted doors and broken background—I wanted to spend my life getting to know her more.

And I did. I spent time with her. I listened to her stories. I met her family. I watched how she treated strangers. I saw how she prayed. I asked questions. I leaned in. I learned her heart. We don't marry strangers. We don't follow people we don't trust, and we don't trust people we don't know. So, how do we say we're following Jesus . . . without ever opening his Word?

Jesus said, *"My sheep listen to my voice; I know them, and they follow me"* (John 10:27). Listen. Know. Follow. In that order. Following Jesus doesn't start with doing; it starts with listening.

You can't follow someone you don't know, and you can't know someone you never listen to. That's why Jesus speaks through His Word—so we can know His heart, not just His commands. Some of us are trying to follow a Savior we barely recognize. That's like taking directions from a stranger—you'll get lost fast.

But when you listen, you begin to know Him. And when you know Him, following stops feeling like pressure and starts feeling like love. Before Jesus said, *"Follow me,"* He spoke. And they listened.

## Avoiding the Bible Means Avoiding Jesus

Let that land. If the Bible is how Jesus speaks . . . then ignoring it is ignoring Him. I'm not talking about legalism here. This isn't about earning gold stars on God's chart. He's not in heaven shaking His head because you hit snooze instead of opening your Bible. God doesn't love you less when you miss a quiet time. But let's be real; relationships don't grow without communication.

Imagine telling your spouse, "I love you; I just don't have time to talk to you . . . ever." Or imagine texting your best friend once a month and expecting to feel close to them. That's not a relationship; that's a subscription.

The Bible isn't about rule-following. It's about relationship-building. And you can't have a real relationship with someone you're not listening to. God is still speaking. The question is—are we still tuning in? And for most of my life, I didn't listen.

I got saved. I believed. I prayed. But I never gave God real access. I wanted salvation without surrender and peace without process. I wanted Jesus as Savior, but not as Lord. That might sound familiar, and you'll see it more than once in these pages—not because I forgot I already said it, but because it's the heartbeat of my story. It's the tension so many of us live in without realizing it. We want the rescue without the relinquishing. But acknowledging Christ's lordship means giving up control. And I didn't want to surrender what I thought was keeping me safe, even though it was the very thing that was keeping me stuck.

And for a guy who grew up with chaos, giving up control felt like inviting the pain back in.

## Giving Someone Control

Giving someone control means putting your life—literally or figuratively—into their hands. It's a terrifying act of trust, especially when you realize too late that the one holding the wheel has no business being in charge of anything . . . much less you. I learned that when I was seven.

Now, for the sake of clarity, let me explain something that might get a little confusing. When I say, "my parents," I'm talking about my mother and my stepfather. Both of them were alcoholics. So, when I say, "I was raised in it," I don't mean they occasionally drank. I mean, the smell of alcohol was more familiar than dinner. I mean, the sound of slurred speech was the background noise of my childhood. It wasn't just part of the environment—it was the environment.

One day, we were visiting my aunt and uncle in Los Angeles. My older siblings didn't have to go, which, to me, seemed like the ultimate injustice. They got to stay home and be teenagers. I got dragged along like a carry-on bag.

It should have been a day of playing in the yard with cousins— building blanket forts, sword-fighting with sticks, maybe pretending we were explorers discovering lost treasure in the bushes. You know, normal kid stuff. This was the sixties. We didn't have video games, tablets, or ten hours of YouTube to keep us entertained. Our imagination was the entertainment; dirt and cardboard were deluxe toys.

But I couldn't play. I couldn't even pretend. Because I watched my stepdad start drinking not long after we arrived, and he didn't stop. Each drink made him louder. His laugh was a little too forced, a little too delayed, and a little too scary. His steps turned sloppy. His eyes glazed over. But the worst part wasn't watching him get drunk—it was knowing that eventually, we were going to leave. And he was going to drive us home.

I can't explain the kind of anxiety that puts into a child. Unless you've lived it, you just can't imagine it. You don't have the words for it at that age; you only have the pounding heart, the shaking hands, the quiet prayers whispered in your head to a God you're not even sure is listening.

I kept waiting for someone—anyone—to step in. My aunt? My uncle? Couldn't they see how drunk he was? I was just a kid, and I saw it plain as day. But nobody said a word. Nobody took the keys. And so, we left. Him behind the wheel. My mom in the passenger seat. Me stuck between them—physically and emotionally.

Not long after pulling away, he hit a parked car. Just sideswiped it. And kept going. No stopping. No checking on damage. Just more yelling. He and my mom going at it. Her shouting at him to stop. Him cursing and accelerating. A few blocks later, he hit another car. Harder this time.

Still no stopping. And now, he was trying to get away.

I remember sitting there, pressed into that awful vinyl seat, heart racing, hands clenched in my lap, not knowing if we were going to die or just get someone else killed. The car smelled like cigarette smoke and panic. Then—sirens. Red and blue lights flashing behind us. The police were chasing us.

You don't forget sirens like that. Not when you're seven years old and praying the car will stop. Not when your mother is screaming, "Stop the car!" and your stepfather is flooring it like he's in a getaway scene from a bad movie. He finally crashed again—this time at the end of a dead-end street. No more running.

Suddenly, we were surrounded. Police cars. Officers yelling. Guns drawn. The kind of chaos you don't forget. They were barking orders like it was a hostage situation. And I guess, in some ways, it was.

They dragged him out of the car. Then my mother. Threw them both to the ground. And me? I just sat there. Shaking. Frozen in place like a statue of fear. I couldn't move. Couldn't cry. Couldn't speak. Just watched everything happen like I was watching it from underwater. Muffled. Disconnected. Terrified.

Eventually, the shouting stopped. The sirens dimmed. The adults were cuffed and placed in police cars.

And I was still sitting in that front seat. Alone. Then, out of nowhere, a giant of a police officer leaned in through the open door. He didn't bark orders. He didn't yank me out. He smiled. Just a calm, gentle smile. Like he knew everything I'd just seen. Like he'd seen it before.

He said softly, "You're okay. I gotcha." And he held out his hand. I couldn't say a word. I just reached for it. And when he lifted me out of the car and into his arms, I buried my head into his shoulder. I don't know how long he held me. But I remember feeling safe. Not something I was used to as a child.

I didn't understand it at the time, but looking back, I can tell you—that was the moment I gave up control without meaning to. Because I didn't have a choice. When you're seven and scared and shaking, you don't get to vote on who's in charge. You just hope someone shows up who knows what they're doing.

That officer did. He didn't try to fix everything. He didn't explain or excuse anything. He just held me. "You're okay. I gotcha." That was enough. But something else happened that day, too—something deep, even if I didn't have the words for it at age seven.

I didn't stand up and declare it. I didn't know how to process it. But something inside me flipped. It was a silent vow. The kind only a scared little kid makes when he's stuck in the middle seat of a moving disaster. "That will never happen again."

Of course, I was seven. I couldn't exactly go get a job, buy my own car, and apply for emancipation. I couldn't even reach the pedals, let alone drive. But in my little-boy heart, I decided one thing for sure: I will never feel this helpless again.

No more depending on people who shouldn't be trusted with goldfish, let alone children. No more riding shotgun in chaos. No more being the kid who just sat there, shaking, while grown-ups made terrible choices. Someday—I didn't know when—but someday, I'd be the one in charge. I'd make the plans. I'd take care of myself. I'd never again be that weak little boy.

And for a long time, I lived like that vow was my compass. I built walls. I smiled at the right times. I tried to look strong, stay sharp, stay busy, and stay ahead. But here's the truth that took me decades to admit, even to myself: That little boy? He never left. He's still in here. And now and then, I still hear him—his voice small but sharp:

"Coward."

"You just sat there and shook."

"You did nothing."

That voice doesn't shout, but it stings. It says fear means failure. That being scared means you weren't enough. That silence is weakness.

But that's a lie. A loud one whispered in a quiet voice. Because here's what I understand now—something that little boy couldn't have known: It's not cowardly to be scared; it's human. And sometimes the most courageous thing you can do is to admit you're not in control . . . and trust the One who is.

That day, God didn't show up with a lightning bolt or a booming voice from the sky. He showed up in the form of a big police officer with a calm smile and a steady voice. "You're okay. I gotcha." He didn't yank me out. He didn't shout orders. He just reached out his hand. And in the middle of my shaking, I grabbed it.

He held me. He didn't ask me to explain. He didn't ask me to be brave. He just held me like I was worth rescuing. That was God. I didn't know it at the time, but now I do. Looking back, I can see it. I hear his voice behind that officer's calm assurance. "You're okay. I gotcha."

And even now—when adult life starts spiraling and the old panic creeps in—when I find myself gripping the wheel of life so tight that my knuckles go white, I try to remember that whisper. Because surrender isn't weakness. Surrender is trust. And maybe— just maybe—that trembling little boy wasn't a coward after all. Maybe he was just doing the bravest thing he could. Surviving . . . waiting . . . Trusting . . . without even knowing it.

Psalm 18:16 says, *"He reached down from on high and took hold of me; He drew me out of deep waters."* That officer, in that moment, was Jesus. I didn't see it at the time, but I know it now. I was stuck in someone else's mess, paralyzed in fear, unable to cry, too ashamed to move — and Jesus showed up with gentleness and strength. Not to punish. To protect. Not to accuse. To assure. "You're okay. I gotcha."

That's what Scripture does. It doesn't just sit quietly on your nightstand collecting dust. It moves. It reaches into the chaos, right into your panic, confusion, fear, and shame—and it pulls you into peace. Not by giving you perfect answers, but by reminding you of who God is right now, in the middle of your mess.

It doesn't ask you to clean yourself up before opening it. It doesn't shame you for not having read it in a while. It simply says, "Here I am. Let me show you the truth." That's why we need God's Word:

- When life gets loud, Scripture speaks louder—but with a whisper that calms the storm instead of adding to the noise.
- When your thoughts race, Scripture slows them down.
- When your past screams, "You're not enough." Scripture gently answers, "But God is."
- When the little voice inside you says, "You'll never be okay." God's voice in His Word says, "You're already mine."

The Bible is not just a book; it's a lifeline, a flashlight in the dark, a rescue rope in the flood. It's a steady hand reaching into your story and saying, "You're okay. I gotcha."

## So Why Should We Read the Bible

We should read the Bible because it's a rescue letter, not a rule book:

- The God who made you wants to speak with you. *"Call to me and I will answer you and tell you great and unsearchable things you do not know"* (Jeremiah 33:3).
- The Savior who died for you wants to walk with you. *"To this you were called, because Christ suffered for you, leaving you an example, that you should follow in his steps"* (1 Peter 2:21).
- The Spirit who lives in you wants to guide you. *"But when he, the Spirit of truth, comes, he will guide you into all the truth"* (John 16:13).
- You're in a war. *"Put on the full armor of God, so that you can take your stand against the devil's schemes"* (Ephesians 6:11).
- Your soul gets hungry. *"Man shall not live on bread alone, but on every word that comes from the mouth of God"* (Matthew 4:4).
- Your heart needs healing. *"He heals the brokenhearted and binds up their wounds"* (Psalm 147:3).
- Your mind gets cloudy. *"Do not conform to the pattern of this world, but be transformed by the renewing of your mind"* (Romans 12:2).
- Your shame needs washing. *"If we confess our sins, he is faithful and just and will forgive us . . . and purify us from all unrighteousness"* (1 John 1:9).
- Your pride needs breaking. *"God opposes the proud but shows favor to the humble"* (James 4:6).
- Your future depends on it. *"Your word is a lamp for my feet, a light on my path"* (Psalm 119:105).
- It's not just a book—it's breath. *"All Scripture is God-breathed"* (2 Timothy 3:16).

Hebrews 4:12 says, *"For the word of God is alive and active. Sharper than any double-edged sword . . . it judges the thoughts and attitudes of the heart."* The Word of God is alive, active, sharp. It is not dusty, not outdated. It's not just words . . . it's Word.

## Don't Wait

Don't wait until your life is falling apart.

Don't wait until you're on the floor crying out, wondering why you feel far from God.

Don't wait until Sunday.

Don't wait until it makes perfect sense.

Open it now.

Ask God to speak—and He will.

Maybe through a verse you've read a hundred times.

Maybe through a line that feels like it was written just for you.

Because maybe it was.

Ephesians 6:17 says, *"Take the helmet of salvation and the sword of the Spirit, which is the word of God."* The Bible is your sword. Don't bring a spoon to a sword fight. Don't walk into war unarmed. Pick it up. Train with it. Let it strengthen your grip.

## Take Off the Bib and Put On the Apron

We've got to grow up. No more waiting to be spoon-fed once a week at church. You're not a baby bird, and your pastor isn't your personal Uber Eats. Take off the bib. Put on the apron. Get in the Word. Let God equip you.

*"All Scripture is God-breathed and is useful for teaching, rebuking, correcting, and training in righteousness, so that the servant of God may be thoroughly equipped for every good work"* (2 Timothy 3:16–17). God's Word is useful; it is not optional or outdated.

You're still here, and that tells me something powerful: You want more. You're hungry for truth—the kind of truth that can't be found scrolling social media or chasing opinions, but only in the unchanging Word of God.

We all need truth spoken into our lives, especially when we'd rather avoid it. And the best place to find real, reliable, life-changing truth is in Scripture—God's own words that cut through confusion and reveal what's real.

So, let's dig in together.

Next, we'll face the raw, soul-piercing reality of truth in two stories that will challenge and inspire you: Jesus standing before Pilate, declaring who He is even when it cost Him everything, and Peter confessing Jesus as the Christ, a moment of revelation that changed everything for him—and for us.

If you've ever wondered what it looks like to stand firm in truth, to speak it, to live it, these stories are for you. Let's turn the page and face the truth together.

# Chapter 5:
# THE LIGHT THAT NEVER LIES

## Jesus before Pilate – The Story

*God's light doesn't just reveal the path; it exposes every lie and leads us with a truth that never changes.*

The sun was barely rising over Jerusalem when Jesus, bound and exhausted, was dragged to Pilate's headquarters. The religious leaders stayed outside to avoid ceremonial uncleanness before Passover, forcing Pilate, the Roman governor, to shuttle between the scheming priests and the silent prisoner. The irony was thick: Men obsessed with ritual purity were orchestrating the murder of the sinless Son of God.

Pilate eyed Jesus skeptically and asked, *"Are you the king of the Jews?"* (John 18:33). Jesus's calm gaze met Pilate's as he asked, *"Is that your own idea, . . . or did others talk to you about me"* (John 18:14)? Pilate snapped back defensively, *"Am I a Jew? . . . . Your people handed you over. What have you done"* (John 18:35)?

Jesus answered with words that revealed both the nature of his kingdom and the futility of human power: *"My kingdom is not of this world. If it were, my servants would fight. . . . But now my kingdom is from another place"* (John 18:36). Pilate latched onto the word *king* like someone trying to win an argument by twisting your last sentence. *"You are a king, then! said Pilate."* In response, Jesus declared with breathtaking clarity: *"You say that I am a king. In fact, the reason I was born and came into the world is to testify to the truth. Everyone on the side of truth listens to me"* (John 18:37).

These words cut deeper than any sword. Jesus was not only asserting his authority but exposing every lie the world uses to justify pride, violence, and rebellion against God. Pilate, face to face with Truth Himself, cynically muttered, *"What is truth"* (John 18:38)? But Pilate didn't wait for an answer; he turned away, symbolizing every heart that chooses comfort over conviction.

Trying to release Jesus, Pilate offered the crowd a choice: Jesus or Barabbas, a violent rebel. Shockingly, the crowd shouted for Barabbas because apparently, "Let's free the violent guy" was trending that day. Pilate, desperate to satisfy them without condemning an innocent man, ordered Jesus flogged. Roman soldiers twisted a crown of thorns and pressed it onto His head, mocking Him with cruel laughter: *"Hail, king of the Jews"* (John 19:3). Blood streamed down His face as they struck Him and spat on Him.

Pilate presented Jesus to the crowd, hoping pity would win the day: *"Here is the man"* (John 19:5)! But the chief priests screamed louder: *"Crucify! Crucify!"* Pilate pleaded again, but fear of a riot and threats to his position finally broke his resolve. Even as Pilate sat in the judgment seat, his power was a facade; the real authority belonged to the One standing silently before him.

Jesus, bruised yet unbroken, told Pilate plainly: *"You would have no power over me if it were not given to you from above"* (John 19:11). His words revealed both God's sovereignty and Jesus's willing submission to the Father's plan. Despite knowing that Jesus was innocent, Pilate handed Him over to be crucified, choosing political safety over the truth he knew in his heart.

## What Can We Learn from Pilate's Story?

Truth isn't just a principle or a perspective—it's a person: Jesus Christ. And in one of the most defining moments in human history, Truth stood trial before power. Jesus, bruised and silent, faced Pilate not as a victim but as a willing Savior. He wasn't there to escape judgment; He was there to carry it for us. His silence wasn't weakness; it was strength under submission. It was purpose in motion.

Jesus made it clear: "*The reason I was born and came into the world is to testify to the truth*" (John 18:37). But Pilate, like so many today, responded not with curiosity, but cynicism: "*What is truth*" (John 18:38)? And then he walked away.

That's the tension we still live in—the temptation to avoid truth when it gets uncomfortable and the pressure to keep peace instead of take a stand. Pilate knew Jesus was innocent—he even tried to wash his hands of responsibility, but truth isn't something we can rinse off when it's inconvenient. It demands a response.

God's intention in this moment was far more than a political or religious clash; it was the fulfillment of a cosmic rescue plan, set in motion since Eden. Jesus didn't lose control here in this moment; He surrendered it. He wasn't overpowered; He chose obedience. And as He stood before Pilate, beaten and bloodied, He was carrying the full weight of our rebellion on His shoulders.

This story still matters today because truth still matters—and it's still on trial. In a culture where truth is often reduced to feelings or opinions, Jesus stands as the unchanging standard. His life, His words, and His sacrifice are a call to courage.

We are not neutral observers. We are part of the story. And like Pilate, like the crowd, we face the same decision every day: Will we choose comfort, convenience, and compromise, or will we stand with Jesus even when it costs us something?

Ultimately, Jesus standing before Pilate reminds us that the cross was not a detour; it was the destination. It was the moment when the innocent Son of God was condemned so that the guilty—us—could be set free. Isaiah had prophesied it: "*He was pierced for our transgressions, . . . and by His wounds we are healed*" (Isaiah 53:5). This scene marks the intersection of justice and mercy where worldly power bowed unknowingly to divine purpose.

This was not the end; it was the turning point. The Truth that stood silent that day now speaks through every generation, calling us to live boldly, love sacrificially, and stand unwavering in the light that never lies.

## Peter's Confession – The Story

*Even in my doubts and flaws, I know this: You are the Christ, the Son of the living God—and that truth is my only hope.*

Jesus and His disciples stood in Caesarea Philippi, a place bursting with temples and shrines to pagan gods—monuments to Rome's power, Greek mythology, and Caesar's supposed divinity. Stone idols lined the cliffs; it was a place that screamed, "This is who's in charge here!" Yet amid all that spiritual confusion and noise, Jesus turned to His disciples with eyes that pierced straight through their hearts: "*Who do people say the Son of Man is*" (Matthew 16:13)?

The disciples shifted uncomfortably. They'd heard the rumors. "*Some say John the Baptist.*" one muttered. "*Others say Elijah; and still others, Jeremiah, or one of the prophets*" (Matthew 16:14). The world had plenty of opinions about Jesus, but none of them were enough.

Then Jesus's eyes locked onto Peter, and the question came like a thunderclap: "*But what about you? . . . Who do you say I am*" (Matthew 16:15)? The words hit Peter like a wave. His mind must have raced: What if I'm wrong? What if I say it out loud, and everyone thinks I'm crazy? But something deeper rose up—a fire that burned brighter than his doubts, a conviction planted by God himself.

He took a shaky breath, his voice cracking with emotion, and blurted it out with breathtaking honesty: "*You are the Messiah, the Son of the living God*" (Matthew 16:16). The words weren't polished or rehearsed; they were raw, true, and bursting from the depths of a heart that dared to believe.

Time seemed to stand still. The disciples' eyes widened—some in awe, some in shock. Peter, who often spoke too soon, had just spoken the greatest truth ever uttered by human lips. And Jesus's face broke into a smile that must have felt like the sunrise. "*Blessed are you, Simon son of Jonah*," Jesus declared with His voice full of joy and love. "*For this was not revealed to you by flesh and blood, but by my Father in heaven*" (Matthew 16:17).

Peter's pulse must have thundered in his ears. He, the impulsive fisherman who often stumbled over his words, had just spoken a revelation straight from God. Jesus looked him squarely in the eye and said words that would forever change Peter's life—and history itself: "*You are Peter, and on this rock, I will build my church, and the gates of Hades will not overcome it*" (Matthew 16:18).

Can you imagine what Peter felt? The man who felt like a nobody now heard Jesus call him a rock, a foundation stone for something eternal. Yet almost in the next breath, Peter's impulsiveness returned when Jesus began to explain He would suffer and die. Peter's fear erupted: "*Never, Lord! This shall never happen to you*" (Matthew 16:22)! Jesus's rebuke came swift and sharp: "*Get behind me, Satan!*" Jesus wasn't calling Peter the devil; He was exposing the dangerous human thinking that tries to avoid sacrifice.

This intense moment showed both Peter's extraordinary faith and his very real flaws. But it also revealed a powerful truth: God doesn't need perfect people; He wants people willing to confess Jesus boldly and let Him transform them day by day.

## What Can We Learn from Peter's Confession Story?

Peter's bold confession in Matthew 16:16, "*You are the Messiah, the Son of the living God,*" was more than a spiritual light bulb moment. It was a divine revelation spoken in a place surrounded by false gods, political idols, and religious confusion. In Caesarea Philippi, where Caesar was worshiped as a god and stone idols lined the cliffs, Peter's words cut through the noise of cultural lies like lightning through the fog.

This wasn't just Peter having a good spiritual day; this was God unveiling the truth through a flawed, impulsive fisherman. Jesus made it clear: This revelation didn't come from Peter's intellect or good behavior. It came straight from the Father (Matthew 16:17). And in response, Jesus didn't just commend Peter—He called out his identity and his role in the Church's future. "*On this rock I will build my church, and the gates of Hades will not overcome it*" (Matthew 16:18).

But here's what makes this moment even more powerful: Peter still didn't fully understand everything. Just moments later, he would argue with Jesus about the cross and get rebuked: "*Get behind me, Satan*" (Matthew 16:23)! The same man who boldly confessed Christ also struggled with fear, pride, and control. And yet, Jesus didn't take back his calling.

This is the context we must not miss: God doesn't build His kingdom with perfect people. He builds it with honest ones—those who are willing to declare the truth of who Jesus is, even when they're still working through their own mess.

This story teaches us that faith isn't about flawless understanding; it's about trusting the One who is flawless. God's intention in this scene was to anchor His church not in Peter's personality, but in the unshakeable truth of Jesus's identity as Messiah. And that's still the foundation today.

In a culture that applauds silence and compromise, Peter's confession stands as a challenge to every believer: Will you speak up? Will you name Jesus as Lord, even when the world pressures you to say nothing?

Ultimately, Peter's story is our story. We waffle, we stumble, we speak too soon, we regret what we said—or didn't say. And yet, God still calls us. He still uses us. He still builds his Church through the confession of people who know who Jesus is and are willing to say so.

Peter's declaration didn't just change his life; it helped launch the movement that would carry the gospel to the ends of the earth. In God's unfolding story, that moment is a cornerstone, reminding us that the most powerful thing we can ever say isn't found in theological debate or intellectual mastery. It's in answering one question with conviction: *"Who do you say I am?"*

Chapter 6:

# WHAT HAPPENS WHEN WE READ THE BIBLE?

*When you start reading the Bible, it doesn't just change your mind; it starts changing your memory, your identity, and your direction. God rewrites what you thought was final.*

Before we get too far, let me ask you a simple question: What do you think happens when someone reads the Bible? I'm not talking about skimming a psalm like it's a Facebook meme or flipping to a random proverb like it's a magic eight ball. I mean, really reading it—with open eyes, an open heart, and maybe even a little desperation. I'm talking about the kind of reading where you're not just curious—you're hungry and desperate for clarity, for peace, for answers, for hope.

If you're not sure what to expect, that's okay. I wasn't either. To be honest, I used to treat the Bible like a car manual—something you reluctantly open only after you've tried everything else and smoke is pouring out. And even then, you're mostly flipping through your car manual, hoping the instructions somehow fix what you already broke.

## Dysfunction Destruction

But before I ever got to that place of desperation, something remarkable happened in my family. I watched firsthand what can happen when someone opens the Bible—and believes what it says.

The Bible didn't just bring knowledge. It brought change. It brought Jesus right into the middle of our mess, like light pushing its way through a boarded-up window. Everything that had felt so locked down, so hopeless, started to shift, just a little. A quiet kind of hope began to stir.

It's hard to overstate how dysfunctional our family was. And yes, everyone says their family was a mess, but ours wasn't just "quirky Thanksgiving drama" crazy. Think more like reality show meets demolition derby. We were like a traveling circus with no ringmaster—just emotional clowns, explosive trapeze acts, and the occasional fire. If our family had a motto, it would've been: "Emotions are dangerous, secrets are sacred, and if something breaks, blame someone else."

My mother—God bless her—had been married three times. She was a tiny woman. Petite, beautiful, loving, and tough. Fierce when she needed to be. She loved us; there's no doubt about that. But she was deeply wounded herself. She was undereducated and naïve in some ways; She was doing the best she could while dragging a lot of pain behind her.

At the time, she was married to my stepdad—a functioning alcoholic, though the functioning part felt debatable most days. When he wasn't drinking, which was rare—there were moments I thought I saw something that looked like guilt in his eyes. Guilt for the cruel words, for slapping my mother, for the pain he caused that hung in the air long after he left the room. But those moments were fleeting.

When he looked at any of us kids—kids he was helping to support but not raise, there was a distance. A bitterness. We were his reminder that another man had been here first. And we were never allowed to forget it. Even the word *support* feels generous, like it suggests care or involvement. Truthfully, it was more like we were a burden he tolerated. He would move out, then move back in. When he was gone, a strange peace would settle over the house, but money would get tight. A different kind of stress would take its place—less shouting, maybe, but more desperation. Survival took on layers.

And while his drinking caused most of the chaos, my mother had her own battle with alcohol. She, too, was an alcoholic. Her love was never in question—she was our fiercest protector, but the pain she carried was deep, and the bottle never far. Even when my stepdad wasn't around, the tension never truly lifted. It just changed faces.

We didn't talk about God in our house. Not even in passing. It wasn't that we were atheists; we just didn't bring Him up. Ever. God was like a distant relative nobody invited to the family reunion. There was no church. No Bibles. No prayers before dinner—unless you count, "Lord, get me through this meal." The only time we heard the name "Jesus" was when someone stubbed their toe or dinner was cold.

And then something happened that none of us expected.

## Dysfunction Disrupted

My older sister went on a trip to Oregon when she was seventeen. We figured she'd come back with postcards and overpriced sandals. But instead, she returned with peace.

She had accepted Jesus Christ as her Savior. This was during the Jesus Movement of the 1970s, when revival was popping up in places like coffee houses and beaches. It was like a spiritual counterculture to the counterculture—people trading LSD for the book of John. At first, we laughed. We thought it was a phase. Like mood rings or bell-bottoms.

But it wasn't.

She didn't just go to church. She craved church. She didn't just read the Bible—she devoured it. And her entire demeanor began to change. She had this calm to her. This grace. The same house surrounded her, but it didn't seem to control her anymore. Her words carried peace. Her eyes had focus. Her life, even in the middle of our tornado, had direction.

She wasn't preaching at us. She didn't shove anything down our throats. She just lived differently—and that got our attention. Little by little, things began to shift. My mom, battle-worn and heart-heavy, started going to church with her. One of my sisters followed, then a brother, then another. It wasn't a dramatic revolution. It was subtle. Quiet. But real.

Less yelling. Fewer slammed doors. More grace. More laughter. We didn't turn into the Brady Bunch, but for the first time, peace didn't feel like a stranger.

And me? I watched. I listened. And though I didn't fully understand it, something in my soul breathed for the first time in years.

## Doubt

Eventually, I found myself in a church service. The music hit me first—loud, alive, emotional. It sounded like the kind of rock I loved, only it had a message that pierced through the noise of my life. Then the pastor started talking, and he spoke with the same peace and confidence my sister had been carrying. He said that God was a loving Father, that Jesus had come to rescue us, and that no one was too far gone.

I wanted to feel what they felt. I wanted to believe in the hope they clung to—that something had truly changed. That I was finally safe. But instead, in the few quiet spaces I could find inside myself, I felt something I didn't expect. Not joy. Not peace. I felt confusion.

And beneath that, something heavier. Maybe grief. Maybe anger. I hate to admit that, but there it was.

It wasn't the kind of explosive rage people write about—it was quieter than that. More like a deep ache wrapped in questions. I remember thinking: Where was this loving Father before? Where was He when we were drowning? Why did we have to go through all that? Why did we still have to go through it? Aren't fathers supposed to show up, fix things, and protect?

And then came the guilt. I shouldn't feel that way, right? Here were all these people praising God, celebrating His goodness, and I was sitting there with this knot in my chest. Was I even saved if I felt this way? Did I accept Jesus, or was I just scared of being left behind in the Rapture? Because trust me, they talked about the Rapture—a lot. Like, "it could happen any second." So, part of me said yes to Jesus out of fear.

Looking back now, I realize this is exactly why new believers need support. I didn't know how to ask the questions I was carrying. I didn't know if I was allowed to. I thought I had to hide the struggle so I wouldn't ruin it for everyone else. I should have gone to my sister; I don't know why I didn't.

But the truth is, struggling doesn't disqualify faith. Struggling can deepen it. That's why the Bible says in 1 Thessalonians 5:11, *"Therefore encourage one another and build each other up, just as you are doing."*

I didn't need someone to tell me to smile and sing louder. I needed someone to sit with me and say, "It's okay to have questions. Let's go to God's Word together." I needed someone to remind me that Jesus wasn't offended by my confusion; He invited it, and He understood it. After all, He had scars too.

When we read the Bible—really read it—we find people just like us. David, crying out in caves. Jeremiah, weeping with confusion.

Thomas, doubting. Peter, denying. And yet, God loved them, used them, and met them exactly where they were.

New believers don't need perfect faith. They need honest discipleship. They need a safe place to wrestle with what's real. And they need us, those who've walked a few steps ahead, to remind them: You're not alone. Jesus came for the broken not the polished.

That's what reading the Bible reveals—not just rules but a relationship. Not just theology but a God who walks into messy homes and wounded hearts and says, "I'm not going anywhere."

## Unexpected Redemption

Now, let me tell you something that still stops me in my tracks—something that reminds me of just how far God will go to rescue someone.

Years into adulthood, I got a call from the veteran's home where my biological dad had just been placed. They told me he was dying. My wife and I dropped everything and drove to Northern California. When we arrived, they said he'd been asking for me all day. That surprised me, coming from the man who had spent most of my life telling me that I was useless, that I'd never amount to anything, and that crying was weakness.

I still remember being at his sister's funeral—my aunt's funeral—as a young boy. I had started to cry. He saw me and walked over, pressing his knuckle so hard into the center of my skull that my feet went numb. He looked me in the eyes and told me, "Don't ever cry. Don't be weak." I resented him for that moment for most of my life. Until recently, I thought I had forgiven him, but I hadn't. Not fully.

That moment had changed me. It locked something inside me so tightly that crying became almost impossible. Tears—those simple, human signs of feeling—felt like a weakness I couldn't afford. And for years, my inability to cry haunted me. It's bothered my wife, who's watched me sit stone-faced through moments that should've broken me open. It's bothered me too.

I see other men weep openly in worship or fall to their knees in prayer, and something in me aches—a deep, hollow longing that whispers, "Why can't you let go?" I want that release. I want that kind of raw, honest connection with God. But it's like a dam was built inside me the day my world taught me that emotions were dangerous, and that dam has never broken.

I've prayed—more times than I can count—asking God to soften that hardened place in me. To make me feel again. To give me the freedom to mourn what needs mourning and to rejoice without restraint. Because deep down, I know tears aren't a weakness. They're a sign of trust. They're proof that you feel safe enough to be vulnerable. And I long for that safety, that softness, that surrender.

So, there I was, sitting beside the dying man who had helped shape every jagged edge of my childhood. The man who never once told me he loved me. Never once said he was proud of me. The silence of all those years sat heavy between us, thicker than the hospital air.

A nurse came in quietly, checked his vitals, and leaned close to me. She explained that his heavily medicated state meant he wouldn't be able to respond—that he couldn't speak or open his eyes—but she assured me he could still hear every word.

So, I took a deep breath and did what I never thought I would. I spoke: "Why didn't you ever tell me you loved me? Why didn't you ever say you were proud of me?" My voice cracked, the weight of a lifetime of questions spilling out. He lay there, unmoving, but I kept going, pouring out what I had carried alone for so long.

And then I made a silent promise—one I thought might finally earn his approval. At your funeral, I won't cry. I'll hold it all in. I'll stay strong. Because maybe, just maybe, that would make you proud, even now. I meant it more as bitterness than bravery.

And right then, a chaplain walked in. He asked, "Are you his son?"

"I am," I replied.

He smiled, kind of amazed. "I just need you to know that your dad asked to pray with me last night."

I was stunned. "This man?" I asked.

He nodded. "He wanted to pray for salvation and a peaceful death."

I didn't have words. My wife ran to the car to grab her Bible and began reading Scripture over him as he lay there, unconscious but breathing. He passed later that day.

The nurse pulled me aside. "In thirty-four years," she said, "that was the most peaceful death I've ever seen."

## Bonus Grace

God's grace still floors me. That He would save a man like my father—a man who rejected Him, cursed Him, shut every door for years—and still show up at the end. That's the God we meet in Scripture.

And there's something else I need you to hear—something that still stuns me every time I think about it: Because one young girl— my sister—quietly, faithfully chose to read her Bible and live it out, everything changed.

Her steady witness became a light in our dark and broken family. It wasn't loud. It wasn't flashy. But it was real. And because of that light, two of my mother's ex-husbands—including my stepdad— came to know Christ. Let that sink in. Grown men, hardened by years of dysfunction and regret, were transformed because one girl picked up the Word of God and let it shape her life.

Because of her obedience, my siblings and I were able to give our children something we never had—a glimpse of God's love and grace. Our kids grew up knowing there was a Savior who cared for them, even if we didn't always get it right ourselves. The generational curse of dysfunction didn't get the last word. God did. Because one young girl opened the Bible and believed what it said, a new story began for our family.

So, ask me what happens when someone reads the Word of God? I'll tell you: Chains break, hearts soften, families are restored, and generations are redeemed. That's the power of God's Word when someone dares to read it and live it.

We never know who's watching, listening, and waiting. And we may never see the fruit of our faith in real time. But when we live it—when we read the Bible, obey it, and let it change us—others take notice. Even the hardest hearts can soften.

That's why this book you're reading matters. That's why Scripture matters. It's not just a path to salvation—it's the thing that sustains us after we are saved. The Bible doesn't just bring us to Jesus; it keeps us walking with Him. It teaches us how to endure, how to forgive, how to fight temptation, how to love people who've hurt us, and how to hold on when everything feels like it's slipping away.

Psalm 32:8 says, *"I will instruct you and teach you in the way you should go; I will counsel you with my loving eye on you."* The Bible isn't a relic; it's a relationship. It's not outdated advice—it's God's living Word, reshaping us from the inside out. When we truly read it, generational chains can break, families can heal, and legacies can change. The Bible's truth doesn't just transform us; it plants seeds of faith that can reach future generations.

Our stories meet God's stories in the pages of the Bible, confirming that His promises are still relevant and powerful today. Every time we open the Word, we find we're not alone—God's story is still unfolding, and He invites us to be part of it.

The enemy will do anything to keep you from God's Word, but he can't steal what you refuse to surrender. Open the Bible. Let it speak, convict, and comfort. Let it change your story and your family's story—forever.

If God can use one teenage girl with a Bible to begin healing a family drenched in dysfunction . . . imagine what He could do through you. You don't need to be perfect. You just need to open the Word, listen, and live it. The ripple effect might be bigger than you would otherwise expect to see this side of heaven.

In the next chapter, we'll step back into Scripture to see what happens when lives collide with Jesus: Saul's radical conversion to Paul, and the Philippian jailer's desperate cry that turned into saving faith. These powerful stories from God's Word remind us that He is still in the business of transforming lives today—yours included. Let's dive in together.

# Chapter 7:
# STORIES OF RADICAL REDEMPTION

*When Jesus steps in, who you were no longer defines who you are: He makes you new.*

## Saul's Conversion to Paul – The Story

Not every story of transformation begins with curiosity or quiet surrender. Some begin in rebellion, hatred, or hopelessness. But the Bible shows us over and over—especially in the stories in this chapter that even the hardest heart can be broken open by God's grace.

Paul's story begins as a man named Saul, who was anything but a neutral observer of Jesus's followers. He was their sworn enemy. Saul wasn't just skeptical of Christians; he was obsessed with hunting them down, destroying their communities, and erasing the name of Jesus from Jerusalem and beyond. He was a brilliant Pharisee, trained under Gamaliel, respected and feared for his zeal. Saul was convinced that Christians were blasphemers leading Israel astray, and he made it his life's mission to crush them.

Scripture doesn't hold back: "*Saul was still breathing out murderous threats against the Lord's disciples*" (Acts 9:1). He didn't just disagree with Christians—he wanted them imprisoned or dead. He personally dragged men and women from their homes, broke apart families, and threw believers into prison. His rage wasn't just cold calculation; it was burning, violent hatred. Saul's fanaticism sent shockwaves of fear through the early church, forcing many believers to flee Jerusalem.

And he wasn't content to keep his campaign local. Saul went to the high priest asking for letters to arrest followers of Jesus as far away as Damascus—over 130 miles from Jerusalem—proving his willingness to do whatever it took to wipe out this new movement. Imagine the terror in the hearts of Christians who heard that Saul was coming.

Yet on that dusty road to Damascus, as Saul plotted his next round of arrests, God shattered his murderous plans. A light brighter than the sun exploded around him, and he fell to the ground blind, helpless, terrified. Then the risen Jesus called him by name: "*Saul, Saul, why do you persecute me*" (Acts 9:4)?

This question must have cut Saul to his core. He wasn't just opposing an idea or a group; he was attacking the very Son of God. The persecutor was now face to face with the One he hated, and everything he thought he knew crumbled.

For three days, Saul sat blind in Damascus, his world turned upside down. The man who had stormed into cities to arrest Christians now needed to be led by the hand, utterly dependent on others. He ate nothing. He drank nothing. He waited, broken, desperate. It was a night of the soul.

Meanwhile, Ananias—a believer in Damascus—received a terrifying vision: God told him to find Saul and heal him. Ananias protested: "*Lord, . . . I have heard many reports about this man and all the harm he has done to your holy people*" (Acts 9:13). Ananias knew Saul's reputation as a violent zealot who would stop at nothing to stamp out the faith. But God said, "*Go! This man is my chosen instrument to proclaim my name*" (Acts 9:15). Even as Saul sat blinded by his sin and pride, God was already rewriting his story.

When Ananias found Saul, he called him "*Brother Saul*"—words of grace to a man who deserved none. He laid hands on him, and something like scales fell from Saul's eyes. His sight returned—and for the first time in his life, he truly saw. Saul was baptized immediately, signifying the washing away of his sin and the beginning of a new life.

From that day forward, the man who once stormed synagogues to arrest Christians now stood in those same synagogues boldly proclaiming, "*Jesus is the Son of God*" (Acts 9:20). His preaching grew so powerful that former allies plotted to kill him. The hunter became the hunted. Saul had been transformed from the church's greatest threat to its most passionate ambassador.

His conversion shocked everyone—believers who feared him and enemies who once trusted him. They couldn't believe the man who once "*breathed out murderous threats*" was now risking his life to spread the gospel. But why did this matter so much? Because through Paul's conversion, God made a dramatic statement to the world:

- No one is too sinful or hostile to be redeemed.
- The grace of Jesus is powerful enough to turn hatred into love.
- The gospel is unstoppable—even the fiercest opponent can become its greatest messenger.
- God's plans cannot be thwarted by human rage or resistance.

Paul later described his own story with brutal honesty: "*Christ Jesus came into the world to save sinners—of whom I am the worst*" (1 Timothy 1:15). His life stands as a testament that the gospel isn't about being good enough; it's about a Savior who is good enough to transform even the worst of us.

## What Can We Learn from Paul's Radical Conversion?

Paul's story proves a powerful truth: No amount of sin, hatred, or resistance can stop God's love. Saul wasn't just indifferent to Jesus—he was violently opposed. But that didn't disqualify him from grace. God chose him on purpose to show that salvation isn't earned—it's a miracle.

God called Saul to be His instrument, not just to rescue one man, but to launch a global mission. Through Paul, the gospel reached Gentiles, kings, and Israel. His transformation shows that no one is too far gone, no past is too dark, no heart is too hard. If Paul could be saved and called—so can we. So can those we've given up on.

That's why his story still matters. We all know people who seem unreachable—maybe we've felt that way ourselves. But Paul's life proves that God can break through in a moment and change everything. It gives us hope for our families, friends, and even our enemies. It challenges us to pray boldly and never underestimate what God can do with a surrendered life.

Paul's story also reminds us who we are. We are not defined by our failures but by God's calling. He sees purpose in pain and power in weakness. What others overlook, God redeems.

Paul's conversion wasn't just personal; it changed history. God turned the church's greatest threat into its boldest voice. Through Paul, the gospel spread across the Roman Empire. He planted churches, raised leaders, and wrote letters that still shape our faith.

His life proves that God's mission is unstoppable. He often chooses the most unlikely to carry His message, and His heart has always been for every tribe, tongue, and nation. No failure, hatred, or opposition can stop the plans of a God who delights in redemption. If God could use Paul, He can use anyone—including us.

## The Philippian Jailer's Conversion — The Story

*"In the moment I thought all was lost, I found a hope greater than chains, a peace stronger than fear, and a Savior who saw me in my darkest hour."*

The story of the Philippian jailer begins long before an earthquake rocks the prison—it starts with a clash between light and darkness in the bustling streets of Philippi. Paul and Silas were there on a mission to share the gospel in a city where spiritual forces held tight control. Among the crowds was a slave girl who followed them day after day. She was no ordinary girl; she was possessed by a spirit of divination—a demon that enabled her to predict the future, earning her owners a fortune.

Everywhere Paul and Silas went, this girl followed them, shouting at the top of her lungs, *"These men are servants of the Most High God, who are telling you the way to be saved"* (Acts 16:17). On the surface, what she said was true. But there was nothing holy about her declaration—this was a demonic strategy to confuse and disrupt. By associating Paul and Silas with a spirit the people already revered, the demon tried to distort the gospel message and sow spiritual confusion.

For days, Paul tolerated her constant cries, perhaps waiting for God's clear timing. But at last, stirred by holy indignation and compassion for the girl who was enslaved physically and spiritually, Paul turned to face her. His voice cut through the marketplace: *"In the name of Jesus Christ I command you to come out of her"* (Acts 16:18)! Instantly, the demonic spirit fled, leaving the girl freed from its oppressive grip.

Imagine the shock of the crowd. One moment, the girl shrieked uncontrollably; the next, she was silent, blinking in stunned freedom.

Yet instead of celebrating her deliverance, her owners were furious—their lucrative business of exploiting her spiritual bondage had ended in an instant. Greed twisted into rage, and they dragged Paul and Silas before the city magistrates, accusing them of stirring up trouble and violating Roman customs.

The crowd quickly turned into a mob. Paul and Silas were stripped, beaten with rods, and severely flogged—an unjust punishment meant to humiliate and silence them. Bleeding and bruised, they were thrown deep into the prison's darkest cell, their feet clamped in painful stocks. The jailer, a hardened man likely used to violence and criminals, received strict orders to ensure they never escaped.

But deep in that dark prison, something extraordinary happened: *"About midnight Paul and Silas were praying and singing hymns to God, and the other prisoners were listening to them"* (Acts 16:25). Instead of cursing their fate or plotting revenge, Paul and Silas chose worship, lifting songs of faith that must have sounded like defiance against the darkness itself.

Then God moved. *"Suddenly there was such a violent earthquake that the foundations of the prison were shaken. At once all the prison doors flew open, and everyone's chains came loose"* (Acts 16:26). The jailer woke with horror to see the prison doors gaping open. Convinced the prisoners had fled and knowing that his own death would follow, he drew his sword to kill himself.

But before he could act, Paul's voice pierced the chaos: *"Don't harm yourself! We are all here"* (Acts 16:28)! The jailer called for lights, rushed into the cell, and fell trembling before Paul and Silas. He had witnessed the power of God—first through the demon's expulsion, then through worship in suffering, and finally through a miracle that freed the prisoners yet left them all standing. Conviction overwhelmed him, and he cried out: *"Sirs, what must I do to be saved"* (Acts 16:30)?

Paul and Silas answered with the heart of the gospel: "*Believe in the Lord Jesus, and you will be saved—you and your household*" (Acts 16:31). That very night, the jailer took them into his home, washed their wounds, and gathered his family to hear about Jesus. By dawn, an entire household believed and was baptized. Where there had been fear and death, there was now joy and life, "*because he* [the jailer] *had come to believe in God—he and his whole household*" (Acts 16:34).

Saving a hardened Roman jailer and his entire household, God demonstrated His heart to include every tribe, tongue, and nation in His kingdom. It's a glimpse of Jesus's command in the Great Commission: that the gospel is for all people (Matthew 28:19).

This story also shows God's unstoppable grace: He can use persecution, injustice, or even prison to spread the good news. Paul and Silas's faithfulness under suffering led directly to a man and his family finding salvation. The Philippian jailer's conversion helped plant one of the earliest European churches—a community Paul would later praise in his letter to the Philippians. Through it all, God proved He is sovereign over every circumstance and relentless in His pursuit of hearts.

## What Can We Learn from the Philippian Jailer's Miraculous Conversion?

The story of the Philippian jailer is a powerful reminder that God's grace can reach anyone, anywhere, at any time. It shows us that God has full authority over every spiritual power and that His light can pierce even the darkest corners of our lives. What begins as a scene of injustice and imprisonment turns into a divine rescue mission—not just for Paul and Silas, but for the jailer and his entire family.

God's intention was clear: to use suffering and worship as the backdrop for a miracle. From delivering a demon-possessed girl to shaking a prison's foundation, God revealed that the gospel is for everyone—slave or free, oppressor or oppressed, religious or irreligious. And through it all, we see that every act of faithfulness matters. Our praises in pain and our prayers in the midnight hour can open doors we never expected and change lives we never imagined.

This story is still deeply relevant because many today live in their own prisons of fear, shame, addiction, or unbelief. And just like the jailer, Jesus meets them right where they are. God's power didn't stop in Philippi. It's still breaking chains today.

Ultimately, this story tells us who we are: people pursued by a God who doesn't wait for perfect moments but crashes into our darkest nights to offer freedom. It reminds us that God can use anything—even prison, persecution, or pain—to bring salvation to others. He doesn't just save individuals—He starts a ripple effect of redemption through families, communities, and generations.

The jailer's conversion is a vivid glimpse into God's larger plan. It fulfills Jesus's Great Commission to take the gospel to all people, crossing lines of status, culture, and sin. It shows that no one is too far gone, and no circumstance is beyond God's reach. In that single night, one unlikely man came face to face with the power and presence of God—and it changed everything.

This isn't just an ancient tale of earthquakes and jail cells. It's a living testimony of what happens when we worship through suffering, trust God in the unknown, and boldly share the hope of Christ. And it leaves us with a question: Where might God be writing a rescue story today—in your life or in the life of someone you've already counted out?

God's grace is still pursuing hearts. His truth is still setting captives free. His mission hasn't changed.

# Chapter 8

# WHAT HAPPENS WHEN WE DON'T READ THE BIBLE

*When we don't read the Bible, we start believing lies—about God, about ourselves, about what matters. Silence isn't empty. It gets filled with whatever shouts the loudest.*

We all start somewhere in our faith journey, but what happens when the excitement fades, and the pages of the Bible begin to collect dust? It's easy to get comfortable with just knowing about God without truly knowing Him. In this chapter, I want to be honest about what happens when we stop reading the Bible—or fail to read it at all—not just the missed opportunities, but the real consequences that show up in our lives, relationships, and spiritual health.

Because here's the truth: Without God's Word, we're navigating life in the dark. And sometimes, it takes hitting a breaking point before we realize how far we've drifted.

Let me share what that looked like for me, and why not reading the Bible was the biggest barrier to fully surrendering my life to God.

## In Control

By the time I had been a believer for over ten years, I had a beautiful wife, two amazing young daughters, a stable job, and more blessings than I could count. On paper, I was doing great. I was a Christian man with a Christian family living a Christian life. But one thing was still missing: I had never fully surrendered to God.

Oh, I wanted the salvation part—absolutely. But the surrender? That was a whole different conversation. I had spent a decade giving God most things . . . while still trying to keep control over the parts of my life I wasn't ready to let go of. And reading the Bible? That didn't exactly make the top of the priority list.

I'd open the Bible occasionally, trying to muscle through chapters that confused me, bored me, or made me wonder if maybe the whispers of "he could have brain damage" were finally catching up to me. I mean, if there were a spiritual SAT, I would've been the kid in the back circling "C" and hoping for the best.

And pride? Oh, it showed up like it had a reserved seat. I wasn't about to tell anyone I was struggling to read Scripture. After ten years of following Jesus, how could I admit I still didn't know how to read His Word—like really hear it, understand it, live it?

I mean, I knew the basic stories—Moses and the Red Sea (which I once mistakenly called the Red River), Abraham being the father of many nations, and Jesus dying on the cross. I could hold a decent conversation about the Bible. But deep down, I knew the truth: I didn't really know the Bible. Worse, I wasn't even trying to learn consistently.

I was saved but not surrendered—still convinced I was in charge, still trying to live for God . . . on my terms. And let me tell you, that approach works about as well as trying to push-start a car in neutral: It goes nowhere fast.

## Break Glass for Emergency

It wasn't until my marriage started falling apart that things began to shake loose. God had done so much for me already, and I was still giving Him crumbs. I had been treating my relationship with God like it was just one part of my life, instead of the center of everything. I'd say a prayer when things got bad, sure. When money was tight, when I thought I might lose my job, when I was desperate for understanding, I'd pray then. God and I were close . . . if by "close" you mean I called Him during emergencies.

But that was the extent of it. I wasn't reading. I wasn't growing. I wasn't surrendered. And the cracks were showing. My marriage was crumbling under the weight of my neglect, both emotionally and spiritually. So, in a moment of clarity (or desperation), my wife and I agreed to see a counselor (she said we were going to see a counselor). Now, I expected some talking about communication or maybe how to split chores better, but the counselor surprised me.

He looked me dead in the eye and asked, "Who is your wife?"

Confused and slightly annoyed, I replied, "She's my wife."

He asked again. "No. Who is she?"

"She's the woman I married. The mother of my children. The person I chose to do life with."

Still, he pressed. "But who is she to you?"

I didn't have a good answer. I shifted uncomfortably in my chair, staring at the floor, feeling like a kid caught cheating on a test. Because deep down, I knew the truth: I'd kept pieces of myself locked away, even from the woman I'd promised my life to. Pieces shaped by pain, fear, and a belief that vulnerability would only bring more hurt.

That's when the counselor leaned forward, his voice calm but piercing: "She should be your best friend. The person you trust with things you've never told anyone. You should be sharing your soul with her. That's the kind of relationship that transforms a marriage."

His words hit like a freight train. They shattered the excuses I'd built around my silence. I realized marriage wasn't about surviving side by side or playing roles: It was about being fully known and still fully loved, about letting someone see the scars you've tried to hide and choosing to trust them anyway.

"When was the last time you let someone see all of you, not the church version, but the scarred, scared version?"

That day, something shifted inside me. I saw that true intimacy wasn't just physical or polite conversation. It was letting down my guard. It was inviting my wife into the dark corners of my story—the places I was sure would drive her away. And it was believing that love could meet me there, heal what was broken, and build something stronger than I'd ever dared to hope for.

It hit me like a ton of bricks. I had been keeping her at arm's length, even while sharing a home, a life, and a family. And it was destroying us.

So, I began to open up. I told her things I was scared to say out loud. I let her see my insecurities, my failures, my past. And instead of turning away, she embraced me. She loved me through it. And in return, she began to share more of herself. Suddenly, our marriage wasn't just surviving—it was healing. Growing. It was in that process that something clicked for me spiritually, too.

That level of intimacy, vulnerability, and trust I learned with my wife—that's exactly the relationship God wants with us. And you can't have that kind of relationship with someone you only talk to when there's a crisis. You can't be close to someone when you avoid their words. God wants us to know Him. And He's already shared His heart with us through His Word.

That's what Scripture is: God's story, God's heart, God's voice. And I had been ignoring it.

## Lamp Light

Psalm 119:130 says, "*The unfolding of your words gives light; it gives understanding to the simple.*" That verse hit different when I realized I was the "simple" one. I wasn't supposed to figure it out on my own. His Word was supposed to light the way. But you can't get that light if you're not willing to open the lamp.

Without the Bible, I didn't know Him. I knew about Him, but I didn't know Him. It's like showing up to your best friend's birthday party and forgetting their name. You might be smiling, dressed up, holding a gift, but if you don't know their name, you're not really that close.

The Bible isn't optional for a thriving relationship with God. It's the foundation. Without it, we rely on secondhand knowledge. And secondhand knowledge can get dangerous. That's when we start believing half-truths or cultural slogans we think are Scripture ("God helps those who help themselves"—yeah, not in the Bible).

Hosea 4:6 says, "*My people are destroyed for lack of knowledge.*" They weren't destroyed because they didn't love God or because they didn't want Him; they were destroyed because they didn't know Him.

What happens when you don't read the Bible? You miss out on the voice of God. You miss out on the truth that anchors you. You miss out on the strength that carries you. And worse, you start substituting God's Word with whatever sounds spiritual.

I was the spiritual leader of my household . . . or at least I was supposed to be. But my wife was doing the heavy lifting, spiritually. I was sending our daughters to Sunday School, sure. They were learning Bible verses. They had the stories. But I wasn't modeling what it looked like to be in love with God's Word. I was raising kids to know about God, while still avoiding getting to know Him myself.

I was unequipped—not because I didn't believe but because I wasn't being trained. Hebrews 5:13–14 says that those who live on milk are still spiritual infants, unacquainted with the teaching about righteousness. But solid food—real, life-changing truth—is for the mature. And how do you get there? *"By constant use,"* it says. That hit me. I wasn't growing because I wasn't using what God had given me. I wasn't in the Word consistently. I was still on milk, hoping for steak-level strength.

It's wild. I would never let my marriage fall apart again without doing something about it. I knew I needed help, and I sought it out. But what about my relationship with God? I didn't have that same urgency. I didn't see the cracks, but I thought I was "good enough." I was a believer. I prayed. I showed up at church. I believed in Jesus.

## Broken and in Need

But I wasn't in a relationship with Him. I hadn't surrendered. I didn't trust Him with all of me. And here's what I finally realized: You can't live for God on secondhand knowledge. You can't grow by outsourcing your intimacy. You can't thrive spiritually when you avoid the source of life.

Even after all God had done—healing our marriage, protecting our family, blessing us far beyond what we deserved—I still wasn't in His word. I tried harder, yes. I'd pick up the Bible more often. I'd wrestle through it. But it still wasn't clicking. Why? Because I still hadn't surrendered. I hadn't let go. I was doing it out of obligation or guilt, not out of desperation or love.

God had more work to do in me. Psalm 119:11 says, *"I have hidden your word in my heart, that I might not sin against you."* I hadn't hidden anything. The Word wasn't even on my nightstand, much less in my heart.

The truth is, sometimes God allows us to be uncomfortable, not to punish us, but to invite us. Not reading the Bible left me spiritually weak. And God, in His love, wasn't about to leave me that way. He had a plan to change me. He has a plan to change you, too.

- Sometimes, before you can be used, you have to be changed.
- Sometimes, before you can lead, you have to be broken.
- Sometimes, before you can love His Word, you have to realize how much you need it.

Eventually, I would learn the power and purpose of Scripture. But not because someone convinced me to. God had to let me walk through some things. He had to let me come to the end of myself. Because surrender isn't a checkbox—it's a process. And it starts when you finally say: "God, I want all of You. Not just the parts that fit into my schedule."

Jeremiah 29:13 says, *"You will seek me and find me when you seek me with all your heart."* All your heart. Not just Sunday mornings. Not just in emergencies. Not just when you feel like it.

All. Your. Heart.

When we stop reading the Bible, we stop hearing God clearly. And when we stop hearing God clearly, we start listening to everything else: our fears, our pride, our culture, our comfort zones, and our favorite excuses (like "I'll read tomorrow. . . probably . . .").

But when we open His Word, everything changes:
- We see His character.
- We remember His promises.
- We learn His ways.
- We fall in love with the One who loved us first.

I'll be honest: I still had a long way to go. But I wasn't alone. God was with me, and He was determined to get my attention—not because He was angry, but because He loved me too much to leave me stuck in my spiritual rut. He wanted my whole heart. And He knew I wouldn't give it until I stopped clinging to control and surrendered.

Friend, if you've been trying to follow Jesus without reading His Word, I get it. I've been there. But don't stay there. God has more for you—not just in eternity, but right now. In your marriage. In your parenting. In your calling. In your everyday, normal life.

And here's the key. It all begins with surrender. That's where transformation happens. That's where faith stops being a title and starts becoming a testimony. That's where the real walk begins.

But here's the crazy thing about us humans: We can see God move mountains right in front of us—and still dig in our heels. We're spiritual toddlers with our arms crossed, whispering, "You're not the boss of me." Don't believe me? You will. Because in the next chapter, we're going to see just how stubborn we can be—even when God makes His power impossible to ignore.

We'll look at the Israelites, who watched the Red Sea split and bread fall from heaven, yet they stayed defiantly stuck in their complaints and fears. Then we'll meet Jonah, who heard God's clear call, ran the other way, and still thought he knew better—even from the belly of a giant fish.

If there's one thing these stories show us, it's that defiance isn't a new problem, and God's patient love isn't either. So, buckle up. Let's dive into what happens when we see miracles but still refuse to follow—and discover how God's grace meets even the most stubborn hearts.

# Chapter 9:
# SILENT RESISTANCE

*When gratitude fades, chronic discontent grows, and no blessing will ever feel like enough until our hearts rest in God.*

## Israel Grumbles in the Wilderness – The Story

Israel had barely dried off from crossing the Red Sea when the grumbling began. One minute, they were singing praises to the God who split the waters and drowned Pharaoh's army; the next, they were side-eyeing Moses with a look that said, "So, . . . what's for dinner?"

Just three days into the wilderness journey, their waterskins ran dry, and they found bitter water at Marah. Their first official complaint meeting commenced: "*What are we to drink*" they whined (Exodus 15:24)? Moses, probably thinking, "You've got to be kidding me," cried out to God, who miraculously made the water sweet. Problem solved—at least for five minutes.

But soon the desert heat turned their thoughts to food. Suddenly, slavery in Egypt looked like a buffet. They wailed dramatically, "*If only we had died by the Lord's hand in Egypt! There we sat around pots of meat and ate all the food we wanted*" (Exodus 16:3). (Which is hilarious, considering they'd been beaten and crying out for rescue just weeks earlier!)

God, infinitely patient, rained down bread from heaven—manna, small white flakes that tasted like wafers with honey. Each morning, they collected it, and every evening He provided quail until it practically piled up knee-high. But the honeymoon with manna ended quickly. Soon they sighed, "Manna for breakfast. Manna for lunch. Guess what's for dinner? Manna."

The grumbling rose to a crescendo in Numbers 11. They moaned, *"If only we had meat to eat! We remember the fish we ate in Egypt at no cost—also the cucumbers, melons, leeks, onions, and garlic"* (Numbers 11:5). (They somehow forgot the whips, forced labor, and genocide.) Moses nearly had a breakdown: *"Did I conceive all these people? . . . Where can I get meat for all these people?"* (Numbers 11:12–13). God answered by sending quail for them to eat until it came out of their nostrils (Numbers 11:20), which is both hilarious and horrifying.

When they reached the edge of the Promised Land, God told Moses to send spies. Ten of the twelve spies returned trembling, focused on giants rather than God's promise. The people flipped out: *"Why is the Lord bringing us to this land only to let us fall by the sword"* (Numbers 14:3)? They even proposed electing a new leader to take them back to Egypt—imagine that political campaign: Vote for me, and we'll march straight back to slavery!

Their chronic discontent revealed hearts addicted to fear, nostalgia, and complaints. They'd seen God split the sea, rain bread from heaven, and defeat enemies—yet they couldn't stop whining long enough to trust Him.

God's patience ran thin. That entire generation, except Joshua and Caleb, was sentenced to wander the wilderness for forty years until they died. Only their children would enter the land they'd rejected in unbelief.

## What Can We Learn from Israel's Grumbling?

It's easy to roll our eyes at the Israelites. I mean, how do you go from walking through the Red Sea to whining about dinner a few days later? But let's be honest—we're not that different. We forget God's faithfulness the moment things don't go our way. One bad day, one missed opportunity, one flashing check engine light, and suddenly it's, "God, where are You?"

Complaining isn't always loud. Sometimes, it's that quiet, disappointed voice in your head: "Why haven't You fixed this yet?" Or the unspoken assumption that today's blessings are just "normal." That's where Israel was—free from Egypt, eating miracle bread, guided by fire and cloud—and still unsatisfied. Why? Because they wanted comfort, not communion.

God wasn't just getting them to the Promised Land—He was shaping them on the way. Daily trust. Quiet surrender. But their grumbling drowned out His goodness. Sound familiar?

We're often surrounded by blessings but too busy scrolling to notice. We ask God for guidance, then ignore His Word. We assume He's holding out on us when really, He's holding us together.

Gratitude anchors us when life feels dry. It reminds us who God is when we can't see where He's taking us. Spiritual forgetfulness didn't stop in the desert—and neither did God's patience.

Ultimately, Israel didn't just need food—they needed transformation. Their failure set the stage for Jesus: not just a provider of manna, but the Bread of Life. Not just a source of water, but Living Water that satisfies forever.

Their story is ours. We're wanderers—yet pursued, loved, and led by a faithful God. So, the real question isn't *whether* we'll face deserts; it's *who* we'll trust in them. And speaking of trust issues, let's talk about a guy who didn't grumble; instead, he flat-out ran. Enter: Jonah.

## Jonah's Refusal – The Story

*"Running from God's call doesn't change His plan; it only delays your peace."*

Jonah's story begins with a command straight from God: "*Go to the great city of Nineveh and preach against it, because its wickedness has come up before me*" (Jonah 1:2). Nineveh wasn't just another city—it was the violent capital of Assyria, infamous for skinning enemies alive and impaling them on stakes. God was basically sending Jonah to the ancient world's version of the mob, and Jonah wanted nothing to do with it.

His response? Pure, unfiltered denial. Jonah didn't debate or ask for clarification; he ran. He headed to Joppa, found a ship bound for Tarshish—2,500 miles in the opposite direction—and paid good money to flee. Imagine him standing at the port, sweating nervously as he bought his ticket: "One ticket as far from Nineveh as humanly possible, please." He wasn't just avoiding God's plan; he was fleeing reality itself.

As the ship sailed, Jonah probably exhaled with relief: "I did it. I'm free." But denial is deceptive. God hurled a storm so fierce that the ship threatened to break apart. Sailors, hardened by years at sea, screamed and tossed cargo overboard, praying desperately. Meanwhile, Jonah? He crawled below deck and fell asleep—an exhausted escape artist hoping to shut out the storm he'd caused.

The ship's captain shook him awake: "*How can you sleep? Get up and call on your god*" (Jonah 1:6)! When the sailors cast lots, God made sure the lot fell on Jonah—His runaway prophet exposed. Jonah confessed: "*I am a Hebrew and I worship the Lord, the God of heaven, who made the sea and the dry land*" (Jonah 1:9). Translation: "Yeah, this whole storm? That's on me."

But even here, Jonah's denial ran deep. He didn't repent. He didn't plead. He told them to throw him overboard, basically saying, "I'd rather drown than go to Nineveh." His stubbornness wasn't a loud tantrum; it was a quiet, deadly refusal to do what God asked.

As soon as he hit the water, the sea went flat calm. The sailors, eyes wide, worshiped the Lord. But Jonah's story wasn't over. God appointed a giant fish to swallow him. Three days and nights in a dark, slimy belly—his personal timeout corner—finally broke his denial. He prayed a desperate, beautiful prayer of surrender: "*When my life was ebbing away, I remembered you, Lord*" (Jonah 2:7).

God commanded the fish, and it vomited Jonah onto dry land. Soaked, stinking, and humbled, Jonah finally obeyed. He marched into Nineveh—probably still smelling like fish guts—and delivered the shortest sermon ever: "*Forty more days and Nineveh will be overthrown.*" (Jonah 3:4). Shockingly, the entire city, from the king to the animals in sackcloth, repented. God, rich in mercy, forgave them.

Instead of celebrating, Jonah stomped outside the city, furious that God had spared his enemies. He built a sulking hut, hoping God might still torch Nineveh. God made a leafy plant grow to shade Jonah's head—Jonah loved it—but the next day, God sent a worm to kill the plant. Then came scorching winds. Jonah, sunburned and angry, told God he'd rather die.

God's final question cut through Jonah's stubbornness: "*Should I not have concern for the great city of Nineveh, in which there are more than a hundred and twenty thousand people*" (Jonah 4:11)? The book ends unresolved—a divine invitation to examine our hearts.

## What Can We Learn from Jonah's Reluctant Journey?

Jonah's story teaches us a hilariously uncomfortable truth: Running from God is like trying to outswim a shark wearing water wings—it's never going to end well. Whether it's our excuses, dramatic exits, or quiet resistance, trying to dodge God only invites storms that rock our own lives and toss everyone in our boat around. Jonah proves that you can't ghost God because He knows exactly where you live.

But God's intention wasn't merely to get Jonah to preach in Nineveh. It was to show that His mercy is so boundless that even the worst people—those we'd rather block or unfriend—are eligible for grace. His purpose was to use even a reluctant "Okay, fine. I'll do it" obedience to bring about life-changing transformation, reminding us that His love is scandalously inclusive. Like a dinner party where you wonder, "How did they get in here?" His guest list is bigger and wilder than our own expectations.

This story remains deeply relevant today because we all have our Ninevehs—places, people, or situations we'd rather avoid than embrace. Jonah's meltdown challenges us to stop sprinting in the opposite direction, to understand that peace doesn't come from getting our way but from following God's lead.

Ultimately, Jonah's journey tells us something both hilarious and hopeful about who we are: Yes, we can be stubborn, dramatic, and even ready to book a boat ride away from God's will, but He doesn't throw up His hands or toss us overboard. Instead, He patiently and persistently pursues us, using even our detours and tantrums to reshape our hearts and reveal His grace.

Jonah's story is also a powerful foreshadowing of God's global mission. It reveals that His compassion extends beyond Israel to all nations, preparing the way for Jesus, the perfect prophet who doesn't run away but lays down His life for God's mission. Through Jonah's reluctance and eventual surrender, we see that nothing—not our pride, our stubbornness, or our excuses—can derail a God whose heart is for every tribe and every person.

# Chapter 10:
# STEADFAST PROMISE

*I didn't need a perfect family; I needed a real one—one built on faith, love, and grace. I gave all I had, even when I feared it wasn't enough. Because in the end, legacy isn't about perfection—it's about leaving behind something honest, something hopeful, and something the next generation can build on.*

K ids from alcoholic, addicted, or just plain dysfunctional homes don't grow up with baby albums and bedtime stories—they grow up with baggage. Emotional duct tape. Survival instincts. They walk into adulthood wearing a well-rehearsed smile and dragging behind them fear, shame, and a desperate need to prove they're enough.

Some eventually crack open a Bible—not as a ritual, but as a rescue. And in those pages, they find something they've never seen: a steady Father. One who doesn't lash out, disappear, or lie. A Father who keeps His promises. They read about screw-ups like David, Jacob, and Peter—men who made a mess of things but were still used by God. And for the first time, they realize healing doesn't mean erasing the past. It means letting God rewrite the rest of the story.

But others never get there. They skim a verse, get confused by Leviticus, and close the Book. They carry their pain into the next generation. They become what hurt them, even while swearing they never would. They build homes in the same fog they were raised in— never realizing the fog doesn't lift until you let the Light in.

Then there are the ones who are stuck in the middle. They want better—better marriage, better kids, better legacy—but never crack open the one book that can help. They're not hostile toward God, just . . . lukewarm. And for the record, Jesus had some strong words for that: "*Because you are lukewarm . . . I'm about to spit you out of my mouth*" (Revelation 3:16). Ouch. But it's not about punishment— it's a warning. Lukewarm feels safe . . . but it keeps you stuck.

Wanting change isn't the same as choosing it. At some point, you have to stop hoping and start hearing. "Faith comes from hearing, and hearing through the word of Christ" (Romans 10:17 ESV). Because what we do with the Bible matters:

- Ignore it, and we repeat the mess we came from.
- Read it—really read it—and we find direction, identity, and healing. Not just for us . . . but for every generation that comes next.

And if you're wondering how I know that: Because I was one of the ones in the middle. Not running from God, not running toward Him—just busy running in circles. I was trying to build something sacred with nothing but broken pieces and duct-taped blueprints.

This chapter is about my plan for a family—a plan I clung to like it was oxygen, even though I had no real idea what I was doing. As I said earlier, I didn't grow up with a healthy model. I wasn't handed a legacy; I was handed silence, shame, and survival skills. My childhood didn't teach me how to lead a family; it taught me how to brace for impact.

For me, it was like trying to write a romantic comedy when the only script I had ever read was a disaster movie. There were explosions, dramatic exits, plot twists that made no sense—and yet somehow, I thought I was qualified to direct a faith-filled family sitcom? Yeah, not exactly Emmy material.

But I was determined. I wanted something better. I wanted my kids to grow up with peace, not panic. I wanted a home where laughter wasn't forced, where love wasn't earned, and where God's name wasn't just mentioned during a crisis. I had the desire—but not the design. So instead of building our family on God's Word, I built it on instinct and impulse. I patched together what I thought a godly home looked like using bits I'd picked up from sermons, Sunday school, and maybe a Hallmark movie or two.

I've mentioned my wife and some of the struggles we faced early in our marriage. And yes, we ended up seeing a counselor. But we didn't go because we were just "going through a rough patch." We went because I had been hiding. Because I had insecurities I never dealt with. Because I was carrying lies, I didn't even know how to unpack, let alone confess. That's why we were there.

I had spent so long trying to look like a good husband that I never learned how to be one. And the truth is, we couldn't move forward until I stopped pretending. So, before I can tell you what God did in that room, I need to take you back. Not just to the start of our marriage, but to the start of my pattern—building a life without fully leaning on the God who gave it to me. And yet—even then—God's grace was already at work.

My wife and I met in church, which, in theory, should be the most wholesome beginning to a love story. And it mostly is.

Except for the part where I initially thought she was dating her brother. (A small detail. Don't judge me.)

See, I met her brother first. So, the night I saw them together at church, I just naturally assumed they were . . . well, together. They seemed to be close; they arrived at the same time, and I wasn't trying to be nosy. I figured, "Nice couple." Turns out, they were family. Which is great, because awkward would've been an understatement.

Anyway, at the end of the service, her brother came over and casually asked if I was heading to the restaurant afterward with the church group. I didn't even know there was a restaurant plan, but trying to sound cool and spontaneous, I said, "Yeah, I'll be there." That's when he said, "Cool—do you mind giving my sister a ride?"

Fate. It just shows up whenever it wants, with no warning and terrible timing. Now, I could write another book about my relationship with cars, most of which were, shall we say, character-building. No doubt you'll remember from an earlier chapter that I once had a car so bad that the doors didn't work, and my wife-to-be had to climb through the window to go on dates with me. (Spoiler: She still married me. That's how I knew her love was real.)

That first night, I happened to be driving my old truck that only had one seat. The driver's seat. That's it—no passenger seat. Just empty floor space where a seat probably lived a long, fulfilling life before giving up on me.

So, I did what any smooth operator would do—I reached in the back, grabbed an old wooden crate, and offered it to her like it was first-class seating. No seatbelt. No cushion. Just a rickety box and blind optimism. But I was so taken by her, I would've risked her spinal alignment for a chance to talk to her. (Romance!)

That night led to another. And another. Then came the three classic stages of Christian dating: the engagement ring, the wedding ring . . .

and, yes—I have to say it—the suffering. (I know, I know. It's an old joke. I shouldn't have included it. But it makes me laugh every time.)

To be fair, the suffering was minimal, and the blessings were many. And I promise—our cars have gotten better over the years. Eventually, she even got her own actual seat, with a seatbelt. I know how to treat a lady.

Our marriage started with a promise. Now, I get it—all marriages start with a promise. That's kind of the deal. Rings, vows, "I do," shared bank accounts, matching towels—the works. But ours started with a different kind of promise. One that came before the altar, before the cake, even before the cheap engagement ring I could barely afford. It wasn't poetic or Pinterest-worthy, but it was real. And it still matters today.

Let me back up. My wife, like me, didn't grow up in a fairy tale. She came from dysfunction—not the sitcom kind, but the kind that quietly shapes your view of love, security, and how quickly people walk away when things get hard. Her story is hers to tell, but we shared something important: We both came from families where divorce was considered normal . . . expected, even. Like it was just part of the cycle. You fight, it gets hard, and then you leave. That's what we saw. That's what was passed down.

But when we started talking seriously about marriage, we also started talking seriously about breaking that cycle. We wanted something different, for us, and for the kids we hoped to have one day. We didn't want to pass that torch of fear, instability, and brokenness to the next generation. We knew firsthand how much it hurt, how much confusion it created, and how hard it was to trust people to stay. So, we made a decision: We were going to fight for this. Even when it was hard. Especially when it was hard.

We talked about raising our children with a foundation in faith. Not just going to church out of habit or guilt, but grounding them in the truth of God's love. We agreed that we couldn't force them to believe, but we could point them to the One worth believing in. That felt like our responsibility. Our legacy.

Now, I wish I could say that all this came from two wise, seasoned adults—but let's be real. We were kids—two young, naïve, wildly in love kids with no clue what kind of battles lay ahead. No idea how heavy life could get. We were full of hope and hormones, making lifetime commitments with barely enough wisdom to do our taxes. But we were sincere. And I loved her with everything I had. I still do.

And she? She loved me in a way that felt undeserved. From the very beginning, I knew she was on my side. Have you ever met someone and just knew they're in your corner? That was her. Even then, I could sense this quiet fierceness in her—like, "Mess with him, and you mess with me." She had a loyalty that didn't just show up when things were good. She's the kind of woman who, once she loves you, there is no fight too great. She doesn't walk away. She digs in.

So, one day, standing in front of her parents' house, I got down on one knee. My heart was racing. Not because I was nervous she'd say no, but because I already knew she was the one, and I didn't want to mess it up. I asked, "Will you marry me?"

She stared at me for a second. And not a quick second. A long one. Like she was reading my soul—or debating whether she could live the rest of her life without seatbelts and functioning car doors. Then finally, with tears in her eyes, she said, "Yes. But on one condition."

Now, you want to knock a man off balance in the middle of a proposal? That's the way to do it. I said, "Okay . . . what's the condition?"

She looked me square in the eye and said, "You have to promise me that if we ever hit a place in our marriage where we want to quit—if we ever feel like giving up—you will look me in the eye and tell me we've done everything possible to make it work. I just never want to quit without knowing we gave it our all."

"I promise," I said. And I meant it with every fiber of who I was. And shortly after that, we were married. She would hold me to that promise.

Had I stopped right then—right after she said yes to forever—and asked God to make me into the kind of husband she needed, I believe so much could have been different. But I didn't. I believed in Jesus. I trusted Him for salvation. I knew I needed Him for eternity. But for everyday life? I figured I could handle that on my own. My attitude was, "God, I've got this part covered. Appreciate the backup."

And so, I led with my instincts instead of His Word. I powered through with my own strength instead of seeking His. I was sincere . . . just self-reliant. I had no idea how much I was missing. I wasn't building on a foundation of truth; I was guessing. Making decisions based on emotion, fear, and what looked good from the outside. I thought good intentions were enough. That love would carry us. That effort could fill in the gaps left by my pain.

It didn't. Because God never asked me to figure it out alone. He asked me to trust Him. To seek Him. To let His Word guide me instead of winging it and hoping I wouldn't mess up too badly. "*Unless the Lord builds the house, the builders labor in vain*" (Psalm 127:1). (And I was sweating, but it wasn't holy labor—it was stubbornness.)

I had no idea how wounded I still was. And I didn't know how much those wounds would affect the people I loved most. My silence. My overcompensation. My quick answers and slow listening. I thought I was protecting them from my brokenness, but really, I was just avoiding it.

And here's what I know now: Avoidance isn't protection; it's delay. What I needed was healing. And healing can't happen if you won't look at what is hurt. God's not afraid of your mess, but He won't force His way into places you're still pretending are fine.

*"Cast all your anxiety on him because he cares for you"* (1 Peter 5:7). Not just the kind of anxiety that comes from bills and deadlines, but the deeper fears. The fear that you're not enough. The fear that if you're honest, people will leave. The fear that you'll repeat what was done to you.

That's what I carried. Quietly. While smiling. While trying to be the kind of husband and dad I never saw growing up. But I didn't know how. And I didn't ask God to show me. I thought being a man meant being strong. But I've learned the strongest men are the ones who know when to fall to their knees.

I was still hiding. Still pretending. Still managing my carefully curated, emotionally duct-taped version of reality. I wasn't just hiding things from strangers—I was hiding things from the people I loved the most. And when you hide things from people who love you, do you know what happens? They ask questions. And when you're hiding, questions feel like an ambush. So, you lie.

Nothing major at first—just little deflections. Half-truths. Casual omissions. But one lie needs another to keep it alive, and then that lie invites three more friends, and before you know it, you're hosting a full-blown Liarpalooza in your marriage.

Now here's the twisted thing about lying: When you lie to yourself, you don't even care if it makes sense. You know it's fake— you just don't want to deal with the truth. Logic is optional. You're the only audience, and you've already decided to believe the fantasy. But when you lie to others? They keep track; they remember the details you forget. And when you slip, and you always do, you get caught. And when trust breaks, marriage starts to unravel.

Trust is the glue in any relationship, but in marriage? It's the foundation. It's not love, romance, or chemistry that holds you together when life gets hard—it's the security of knowing the other person is telling the truth. When that's gone, everything wobbles.

And here's what I didn't realize then: Yes, the truth hurts. But that pain? It has a purpose. Telling the truth can feel like pulling out a thorn that's been lodged in you for years. It stings. It bleeds. But it also makes healing possible. "*Then you will know the truth, and the truth will set you free*" (John 8:32).

But freedom never comes without a cost. The truth sets you free, but first it breaks your pride. What I didn't understand—and what some don't learn until it's too late—is that truth has a window. If you tell it early enough, yes—it causes pain. But it also creates space for healing. Real trust can begin again.

But wait too long? Wait until the lies have taken root? Until your spouse is questioning everything they thought they knew about you? Then you're not just dealing with betrayal; you're dealing with resentment. And resentment is a different beast entirely.

> It doesn't just say, "You hurt me."
> It says, "You kept hurting me—and I stayed."
> It says, "I don't just feel betrayed—I feel foolish."

And rebuilding from that takes a whole lot more time, grace, and surrender. This is exactly what I created in my marriage.

There were things about me that my wife didn't know—things I'd kept tucked away, thinking, "If I just bury this deep enough, it'll never surface." But those secrets? They had fingerprints. They shaped my habits. They shaped my personality. They shaped how I handled conflict, intimacy, trust, and vulnerability. And eventually . . . she noticed.

As hard as I tried to keep everything hidden, the cracks started to show. And she didn't recognize the man in front of her anymore—not because I had changed, but because she was finally seeing the man I had always been underneath the mask. "*Whoever conceals their sins does not prosper, but the one who confesses and renounces them finds mercy"* (Proverbs 28:13). (Mercy doesn't come to the one who hides; it comes to the one who steps into the light.)

So, if you're reading this and you're hiding anything, let this be your warning and your invitation. Don't wait until truth has to be ripped from your hands. Offer it. Lay it down before it costs you the very thing you're trying to protect.

Yes, there may be pain. Yes, you may be misunderstood for a moment. But truth opens the door to healing. And healing can restore what lies destroy. I believe that there is a sacred kind of grace in the moment God lets us see—clearly, painfully, mercifully—what we're about to lose. When He opens our eyes to the damage we've done, not to shame us, but to save us. It's in that glimpse of what was, what could be, and what might never return—that we're given one final choice: to fight for the love we still have or to bury it beneath the wreckage of pride and regret. Some marriages are saved right there, in that last light before the fall. Others aren't. But if God gives you that moment, don't miss it.

God doesn't punish us for not reading the Bible, but sometimes, we punish ourselves by ignoring it. We miss out on the one resource that offers the kind of truth nothing else in this life ever could—the truth that never changes, never expires, and never stops speaking. The Bible isn't just a book; it's an invitation to discover who you are, who you were created to be, why you're here, and what's been waiting for you all along.

So no, I didn't dive straight into the Bible to fix everything I'd broken in those first seven or so years of marriage. I wish I had. But I was still trying to duct-tape things together with pride, performance, and a dash of denial. I was still pretending I could manage the mess without fully surrendering to God. And yet—God, in His grace, still stepped in.

He gave us a resource. A moment. A lifeline. We had hit a rough patch—okay, more like a cliff's edge—and everything we had built was cracking beneath our feet. The lies I told. The habits I formed. The emotional distance I created while chasing an image of strength. I was working so hard to prove I was "the man," I didn't even notice my wife had stopped watching the show.

And she was hurting. Not in a dramatic, throw-a-plate-across-the-room kind of way—but in the quiet kind of pain. The kind that builds over time. The kind that's easy to ignore if you're not paying attention . . . and I wasn't.

She was lonely, insecure, and confused. She didn't recognize the man I had become—because honestly, I didn't either. She felt unseen, unheard, unimportant. And when someone feels invisible in their own marriage long enough, they eventually disappear emotionally, even if they're still in the room.

We had always said divorce wasn't an option. That was our big promise. But now? We were sitting across from each other at one of our favorite spots, talking through how we would divorce—who would get what . . . where the kids would live . . . how the finances would work. Casual dinner conversation, you know. Just splitting up a life we never thought we'd lose.

I got up to use the restroom, still numb, heart pounding, stomach in knots. And on my way back, the DJ—who somehow knew us from being regulars—motioned me over.

"What's up with you two tonight?" he asked. "You're not your usual happy selves."

I shrugged. "We're here to talk about our divorce."

His face dropped. "Man . . . no. Hang in there."

It wasn't much, but it was something. A crack of human kindness in the middle of our unraveling. I went back to the table. We started talking again—more softly this time. Sadness hanging between us like a fog. Then suddenly, the DJ's voice came through the speakers.

"This next one goes out to a very special couple tonight."

And then—of all things—he played The Righteous Brothers: **"You've Lost That Lovin' Feelin'."**

I laughed. Not because it was funny, but because it was exactly what was happening.

We danced. Slowly. Brokenly. Quietly. And in the middle of that moment, my wife pulled back just enough to look into my eyes. And she was crying.

It broke me.

She wasn't supposed to hurt like this. I was supposed to protect her. Love her. Be her safe place. And instead, I had become the source of her pain.

She leaned in and said, "You know what hurts the most?"

I shook my head.

"You promised me," she said, "that before you ever walked away from this marriage, you would fight for me. You told me you'd do everything possible. I trusted you. So . . . have you done everything? Have you fought for me?"

I froze.

That was the moment I thought, *my marriage is over.*

## But God

Let's pause for a second. What should we think when we see the words *But God* in Scripture—or in life? We should pause. We should lean in. Because what comes after those two words is always grace, intervention, and possibility.

Romans 5:8 says, *"But God demonstrates his own love for us in this: While we were still sinners, Christ died for us."* (Not after we cleaned up, not once we deserved it, but while we were still in the middle of the mess.) The words *"But God"* mean the story isn't over—even when it looks like it is. That night, by His grace, He gave me one last glimpse—one last clear picture of what I was about to lose. And instead of letting me destroy it, He handed me a choice.

And He didn't just give me a moment—He gave me a resource. A counselor. Someone to help me see what I was blind to. Someone who helped me stop trying to fix the surface and start addressing what was underneath. And that started with me telling my wife everything. Not just what I had done, but why. The hurt. The abuse. The lies. The fear. All of it.

I was terrified. But she didn't run. She didn't dismiss me. She didn't destroy me. She loved me. More. She allowed me—for the first time in my life—to be someone I had never been before: *me.* That kind of grace only comes from God. And the strength to receive it only comes from someone who remembers a promise, even when they have every reason to toss it out the window. She held me accountable. Not to perfection, but to the vow I made when I asked her to marry me, when she handed me her heart like a fragile piece of fine china and trusted I wouldn't drop it.

And you know what? God does the same. Except He's way more patient—and He doesn't just remember His promises; He invites us to hold Him to them. Even when we panic, try shortcuts, or, like Abraham and Sarah, decide maybe God needs a little help (cue Hagar). Or like Moses, who had the nerve to stand before God and say, "Uh, Lord? Remember that promise not to wipe everyone out?"

We weren't the first to try to hold God to His word—or to wonder if He still meant what He said.

Next, we're going to meet a couple who got tired of waiting and a leader who dared to remind God of His own promises. Abraham and Sarah take a wild detour into DIY family planning, and Moses holds God to His word like the boldest lawyer in history. Both moments show us how God's promises stand strong even when we wobble—and how remembering them can anchor us when life feels like it's spinning.

So, let's open the Word together and see what these ancient promises teach us about faith, patience, and the God who never forgets what He said—even when we do.

# Chapter 11:

# FULFILL WHAT YOU HAVE SPOKEN

*When we rush God's timing, we often create pain He never intended—but His grace can still redeem our impatience.*

## Abraham, Sarah, and Hagar – The Story

God had made an astonishing promise to Abram: "*Look up at the sky and count the stars—if indeed you can count them. . . . So shall your offspring be*" (Genesis 15:5). But as years turned into decades, the stars seemed to mock them. Sarai's empty arms weighed heavier with each passing year, and the laughter they once shared turned into awkward silence. Every month brought another wave of disappointment until bitterness settled into their hearts.

One day, Sarai's frustration boiled over. She called Abram in, her voice brittle with pain: "*The Lord has kept me from having children. Go, sleep with my slave; perhaps I can build a family through her*" (Genesis 16:2). It was a plan born of impatience and desperation—a human attempt to rush God's timing.

Abram agreed, and Hagar, Sarai's Egyptian servant, was swept into their scheme with no voice of her own. Soon, Hagar conceived, and everything changed. She began to look at Sarai with quiet contempt, her pregnancy a constant reminder of what Sarai could never have. Sarai's hurt hardened into rage. She lashed out at Abram: *"You are responsible for the wrong I am suffering"* (Genesis 15:5). He, eager to avoid conflict, told her: *"Your slave is in your hands; . . . . Do with her whatever you think best"* (Genesis 16:6). Sarai mistreated Hagar so badly that she fled into the wilderness.

Alone and pregnant, Hagar collapsed near a spring. That's when the angel of the Lord appeared—not with condemnation, but compassion: *"Hagar, slave of Sarai, where have you come from, and where are you going"* (Genesis 16:8)? God gave her a promise: she would bear a son named Ishmael, meaning "God hears," because God had heard her misery. Hagar named Him "El Roi," the God who sees me—the first person in Scripture to give God a name. The God of Abraham—the big, star-counting, promise-making God—stooped low enough to meet a scared, pregnant, runaway servant. That's who He is. And He sees you, too.

Hagar returned and bore Abram a son. Abram named him Ishmael. But God's promise hadn't changed: Sarah herself would bear the child of promise. Thirteen years later, when Abram was ninety-nine, God appeared again, changing Abram's name to Abraham, meaning "father of many," and Sarai's name to Sarah, meaning "princess." God promised, *"I will bless her and will surely give you a son by her"* (Genesis 17:16). Abraham laughed in disbelief, thinking, *"Will a son be born to a man a hundred years old"* (Genesis 17:17)?

Soon after, three mysterious visitors—angels in disguise—arrived at Abraham's tent. Sarah, eavesdropping behind the tent flap, heard one say, *"I will surely return . . . and Sarah, your wife will have a son"*

(Genesis 18:10). She laughed silently, thinking, "*After I am worn out and my lord is old, will I now have this pleasure*" (Genesis 18:12)? God called her out: "*Why did Sarah laugh? . . . Is anything too hard for the Lord*" (Genesis 18:13–14)?

A year later, Sarah held Isaac—"he laughs"—in her arms. Joy erupted. But the consequences of their earlier plan quickly resurfaced. At Isaac's weaning feast, Ishmael, now a teenager, mocked his little brother. Sarah's old jealousy reignited into fury: "Get rid of that slave woman and her son…" Abraham was torn—he loved Ishmael deeply—but God told him to listen to Sarah, promising Ishmael would also become a great nation.

So, Abraham rose early, gave Hagar and Ishmael bread and water, and sent them into the desert. When their water ran out, Hagar placed Ishmael under a bush, unable to watch him die. But God heard Ishmael's cries. He opened Hagar's eyes to a well, saving them both and reaffirming His promise: Ishmael would father a great nation, too.

The unintended consequences of their impatience were enormous:

- Jealousy and division split their household.
- Ishmael's descendants and Isaac's would clash for generations, fueling conflict that still echoes today.
- The pain of trying to rush God's promise scarred relationships and hearts.

Yet God's faithfulness never wavered. He fulfilled His word through Isaac while still showing compassion to Hagar and Ishmael.

## What Can We Learn from Abraham, Sarah, and Hagar?

The story of Abraham, Sarah, and Hagar teaches us a painfully familiar truth: when we get impatient with God's timing, we start improvising—and our shortcuts usually lead to pain, division, and consequences we never saw coming. Like trying to microwave a gourmet meal, rushing God's process only creates a mess. We do the same thing today when we settle for relationships God never led us to, take jobs He didn't confirm, or make decisions out of fear that nothing is happening.

Abraham and Sarah tried to help God by speeding up His promise. Their impatience produced jealousy, division, and lasting pain—but God's grace still met them there. He is the God who sees (El Roi) and the God who hears (Ishmael). Even when we take detours, He remains faithful to finish what He started.

And here's the hope: God sees and cares for everyone in the story—even those wounded by someone else's impatience. He met Hagar in her heartbreak, called her by name, and gave her a future. These stories remind us that even when we create chaos, God's compassion reaches every corner of the mess.

They remind us to wait, to trust, and to let God's timing be perfect—even when we don't understand it. His promises don't need our help; they need our faith.

## Moses's and God's Promise – The Story

*Lord, remember what You promised—let Your faithfulness triumph over our failures.*

Moses had been on Mount Sinai for forty days and forty nights, enveloped in God's glory, receiving the Ten Commandments—God's very words carved into stone. Meanwhile, at the base of the mountain, Israel grew restless. Fear whispered through the camp: "Moses is gone. Maybe he's dead. What now?"

In desperation and impatience, they crowded around Aaron: "*Come, make us gods who will go before us. As for this fellow Moses who brought us up out of Egypt, we don't know what has happened to him*" (Exodus 32:1). Instead of standing firm, Aaron folded instantly. He told them to hand over their gold earrings; he melted them down and shaped a golden calf. The people looked at the idol and shouted, "*These are your gods, Israel, who brought you up out of Egypt*" (Exodus 32:4).

They offered sacrifices, ate, drank, and danced wildly, abandoning the very God who had just split the Red Sea. While they reveled, Moses stood high on Sinai, unaware—until God's voice thundered:

> *Go down, because your people, whom you brought up out of Egypt, have become corrupt. . . . Now leave me alone so that my anger may burn against them and that I may destroy them. Then I will make you into a great nation.*
>
> —Exodus 32:7, 10

This was a breathtaking moment. God, who is perfectly just, had every right to wipe them out. He even offered Moses a clean slate: starting over with him alone. But Moses, who once begged God not to send him at all, now stood boldly as Israel's advocate. His heart broke for the people—even in their sin—and he dared to plead with the Almighty.

Moses's intercession was anchored not in Israel's worthiness but in God's own promises. He cried out: "*Lord, why should your anger burn against your people, whom you brought out of Egypt with great power and a mighty hand*" (Exodus 32:11)? He appealed to God's reputation among the nations: "*Why should the Egyptians say, 'It was with evil intent that he brought them out, to kill them in the mountains'*" (Exodus 32:12)?

Then Moses reached for the heart of the matter: God's covenant promise. "*Remember your servants Abraham, Isaac, and Israel, to whom you swore by yourself: 'I will make your descendants as numerous as the stars in the sky and will give your descendants all this land I promised them'*" (Exodus 32:13).

Generations earlier, God had spoken to Abraham, Isaac, and Jacob, swearing by His own name that He would make their descendants a great nation, give them the land, and bless the world through them. Moses clung to that promise, believing God could not and would not lie. His plea was bold, almost audacious. In other words, Moses pleaded with God to fulfill what He had spoken, to stay true to His word, and honor His covenant—even though the people didn't deserve it. What if we prayed like that? Not with perfect words, but with bold faith that clings to what God already said. What if our response to failure wasn't shame, but remembering?

Then came one of Scripture's most astonishing lines: "*Then the Lord relented and did not bring on his people the disaster he had threatened*" (Exodus 32:14). God chose mercy over judgment—not because Israel had earned it, but because He is faithful to His promises.

When Moses descended the mountain, tablets of stone in hand, he saw the chaos himself: people dancing around the calf, lost in their sin. His righteous fury ignited. He shattered the tablets at the foot of the mountain—symbolizing Israel's shattered covenant—ground the idol to powder, scattered it on the water, and made the people drink it, forcing them to taste the bitterness of their betrayal.

The consequences were devastating: Thousands died, the Levites executed idolaters, and Israel faced a plague. Yet because Moses dared to remind God of His promises, God did not destroy the nation. Instead, He renewed His covenant and continued His plan through them.

## What Can We Learn from This Story?

The story of Moses interceding for Israel after the golden calf disaster reminds us of something we need to hear: Even when we spectacularly blow it—melting down jewelry into a sparkly cow just days after God split the sea—God still invites someone to stand in the gap with prayers rooted in His promises. It's not about pretending sin doesn't matter; God is holy, and He takes rebellion seriously—but it's about showing that His mercy is always on the table when we come to Him with humility and faith. Moses didn't beg God based on Israel's goodness; he appealed to God's unchanging word and character. It was like saying, "God, we've messed up—big time—but You're still the same God who made a promise. And we're asking You to keep it."

God's intention wasn't to let sin slide, but to reveal His heart: He is faithful even when we are not. He wanted Israel—and us—to understand that His covenant stands firm, even when we chase shiny distractions and forget where our hope comes from.

What we can take away is deeply humbling and wildly hopeful: Our prayers matter. Not because we're persuasive, but because God delights in keeping His word. When we pray, "Lord, You promised . . . ," we're not twisting His arm—we're aligning our hearts with His. This kind of prayer isn't just spiritual lip service; it's standing in the tension between failure and faith, holding onto the truth that God still listens, still moves, and still redeems.

This story is still painfully relevant because people haven't changed. We still get impatient. We still forget. We still build modern-day idols out of jobs, relationships, security, and control. But God still calls us to intercede—for our families, for our communities, and for those who've forgotten His faithfulness. He invites us to step into the mess and say, "God, do what only You can do. Fulfill what You have spoken."

Ultimately, this story tells us who we are: a forgetful people prone to panic and golden calves—but also people who, like Moses, can become bold intercessors. It also shows us who God is: He is unshakably faithful, patient beyond understanding, and always ready to fulfill His promises, even when we least deserve it. And this story points us to Jesus—the perfect Mediator—who stood in the gap not with words, but with His life, so that every promise God ever made would be fulfilled in full.

These stories teach us that God is not fragile—His plans don't break when we do. Whether it's a shortcut we regret or a golden calf we pretend isn't there, His promises still hold. He invites us to trust again, not because we've proven ourselves, but because He already has.

## Chapter 12:
# WHERE GRACE AND MERCY COLLIDE

*Mercy held back what I deserved. Grace handed me what I never could.*

That leads me to two of the greatest highlights of God's Word: grace and mercy. These aren't just fancy church words we throw around before potlucks. They are the heartbeat of God's love for us. Grace is when God gives us what we don't deserve. Mercy is when He holds back what we do deserve. One is like getting a bonus check you didn't earn, and the other is like not getting the speeding ticket even though the cop definitely saw you doing eighty-five in a fifty-five speed zone. (Hypothetically, of course.) The entire Bible is laced with these two things: God lifting people up who didn't earn it and sparing people who blew it. Which means . . . there's hope for the rest of us.

Just in case we try to convince ourselves we have to earn His kindness, God spells it out: *"But God, being rich in mercy, because of the great love with which he loved us, . . . made us alive together with Christ—by grace you have been saved"* (Ephesians 2:4–5 ESV).

It wasn't because we aced some spiritual test or kept our sin under the legal limit. He gave us mercy because He loves us. He gave us grace because He wanted to. That's it. And if you've ever needed a reason to crack open your Bible, let this be it: The One who knows the worst about you still chose to offer you His best. That's not just holy—it's hilariously unfair. And that's exactly what makes it so amazing.

When my girls were little and having what we'll politely call "a moment," we had this old Smash Ball paddle lying around the house. You know the kind—plastic, flimsy, one half of a cheap beach toy set. Well, I repurposed it into something far more intimidating: the Smash-Butt Paddle. It sounds way worse than it was. Let me be clear—yes, there were occasional spankings, but calling it a "swing" would be generous. It was more like a slow, dramatic tap followed by a TED Talk on decision-making.

See, before every spanking, I'd sit them down and explain what was happening. I wasn't interested in just handing out punishment; I wanted them to understand the "why." And sometimes, instead of the paddle, they'd get a lesson in grace and mercy. I'd start like this: "Girls, do you know what grace is?" They'd look up with those wide, suspicious eyes that asked, Is this a trap? I'd say, "Grace is when God gives us something good that we don't deserve." Then I'd give them an example:

"Remember that time Mommy took you to the store and you were acting up like tiny tornadoes of chaos—whining, crying, knocking things off shelves? You just knew she was going to lose it. But instead of snapping, she bought you and your sister ice cream.

Not because you earned it, but because she saw you were tired, overwhelmed, and needed kindness more than correction. That's grace." They usually nodded . . . mostly because they remembered the ice cream.

"And mercy?" I'd say, "That's when you deserve a consequence—like, say, a very light tap from the Smash-Butt Paddle, but you don't get it." And then I'd look at my youngest, who had already mastered the art of theological negotiation. She'd bat her eyes and whisper, "Daddy, can I have mercy today?" Sometimes, I gave it. Sometimes, I didn't. But every time—without fail—she'd follow it up with, "Daddy, before you spank me . . . can I give you a hug?"

Y'all, this kid could've gotten out of a parking ticket in three states. She knew exactly what she was doing. And I knew it too. But here's the thing—I loved it. I loved that she knew mercy was available. I loved that she asked. I loved that her heart stayed soft enough to reach for mine even in discipline. And it made me think: isn't that exactly what God wants from us?

Scripture says, *"But because of His great love for us, God, who is rich in mercy, made us alive with Christ . . . it is by grace you have been saved"* (Ephesians 2:4–5). Rich in mercy. That's the God we serve. Not stingy. Not waiting to whack us with a cosmic Smash-Butt Paddle. But rich in mercy. And like a good Father, He knows when to correct and when to comfort.

Sometimes, God lets us face consequences so we grow. Other times, He gives us ice cream when we deserve the paddle. That's grace. That's mercy. And that's love. The kind that disciplines, yes—but never distances. That was the kind of love I wanted to pass on. So, when we found out we were having a little girl the first time, I was both thrilled and terrified. I knew I wanted her to feel loved consistently, unmistakably. I wanted her to know it, hear it, and see it every day.

But love isn't just what you say. It's what you sacrifice. We didn't have much money at the time, so I sold something I loved— the truck. Yeah, the same truck from our first date. The one with no passenger seat, just an old crate she climbed onto without complaint. I loved working on that truck. But my wife made it clear: "We need a crib more than we need a carburetor."

So, I let it go. And with that money, we got everything ready for our daughter's arrival. And when she was born, and I saw her for the first time—tiny, perfect, and somehow already owning my whole heart—I knew it was worth it. God's grace? It looked a lot like holding her in my arms and realizing that loving her meant letting go of something I loved for someone I loved more.

This is the story of the night I discovered that mercy isn't just what holds back pain—it's what holds us together. At just five months old, our little girl got sick. Really sick. We didn't know what was wrong—we only knew it was serious. She was admitted to Children's hospital in Southern California, and from the very beginning, it felt like we were walking into something we weren't prepared for. They ran test after test. Poked. Prodded. Monitored. Scanned. And after all of it, they still couldn't give us an answer.

I remember standing by her hospital crib, watching my wife sit in the stiff vinyl chair beside it. She cradled our daughter in her arms, rocking gently, humming under her breath. Our baby was crying— uncomfortable, feverish, in pain—but my wife just held her close, whispering and praying, soothing her the only way she could. I stood there . . . and felt completely helpless.

We prayed for answers. Pleaded for something simple. That they'd come back and say, "We found the problem, here's the treatment, and you'll be going home in a couple of days." That's what we were hoping for. But that's not what we got.

Instead, things escalated. Soon, my wife found herself holding our little girl tighter than ever, refusing to let go. As she cradled her, they were surrounded by wires and monitors blinking and beeping softly. An IV was taped to our daughter's tiny foot, delivering the medicine she desperately needed. Doctors began coming in more often. Nurses whispered urgently in the hallway. And my wife could see their faces change—from clinical calm to something that looked a lot like concern. Deep, growing concern.

The longer we waited, the worse it felt. And then came the moment I'll never forget. They brought us into a private room—the kind of room they don't use for good news. The look on the doctor's face said everything before he even opened his mouth.

He sat down and told us, carefully, that they still didn't know exactly what was happening. But her body had stopped producing white blood cells. Something aggressive was attacking her system, and they couldn't yet tell us what it was. Then he said words that made my heart sink: "If we don't figure this out soon . . ." He paused, his eyes heavy with concern. "Things aren't looking good." Just like that.

I don't even know if I breathed after that sentence. My wife grabbed me, and I'll never forget the look in her eyes—wide, terrified, pleading. That look that said, "Do something." She needed me to fix it. To make it stop. To be strong.

But I had nothing. There was nothing I could say. Nothing I could do. I was her protector, her husband, her safe place—and I couldn't fix it. I couldn't save our daughter. And I couldn't save her from the heartbreak of watching it happen.

It's a special kind of pain when you realize the most important people in your life are looking to you for strength . . . and you've run out. I wanted to scream. I wanted to curse the sky and yell at God and demand to know why. Why would You let this happen? Why aren't You doing something?

I didn't need a sermon. I needed a miracle. Everything inside me was shaking with fear, helplessness, desperation. I wasn't thinking about theology or faith or Scripture. I was thinking about my little girl slipping away. I was thinking about my wife crumbling under the weight of it all. I was thinking about how utterly powerless I was as the reality that we could be on the edge of losing everything sank in. There was no strength in me—only pleading. Only pain. And if God heard me, I wasn't sure what He was waiting for.

In that moment—after the doctor told us the seriousness of her condition—I couldn't think clearly. I was frozen, overwhelmed, and drowning in fear. But I knew one thing: I needed help. Not just medical help. Not more test results or another doctor with bad news. I needed someone who knew how to get to God. And I knew exactly who to call.

My brother. He was the one person I knew who walked closely with the Lord. He didn't just talk about God—he knew Him. He was the kind of person who didn't flinch when crisis hit. A prayer warrior. Steady. Anchored. Faithful. And I needed that right now more than anything.

I picked up the phone and called him, my voice breaking as I tried to explain what the doctors had said. He didn't interrupt. He didn't try to calm me down or give me answers. He just listened. And when I finished, barely able to get the words out, he said with quiet strength, "I'll be there. Right now. I'm coming." And he meant it.

I hung up the phone and sat back down beside my wife, who hadn't moved from our daughter's bedside. I wanted so badly to do something—say something that would give her comfort. But I couldn't. So, I did the only thing I could. I stayed. I sat beside her, our hands touching as we watched our baby girl, wires running from her tiny foot, machines beeping steadily, her little body still fighting.

Everything had spiraled so fast. One moment, we were hopeful for a simple answer. Next, we were praying our daughter's condition would suddenly improve. I kept thinking, *How did we get here? How did this happen so fast?* Then I heard something in the hallway. A commotion. Voices—strong, firm, insistent. And one of them was unmistakable: my brother.

I stood up and stepped out into the hallway just in time to hear a nurse saying, "I'm sorry, visiting hours are over. You can't go in right now." And my brother, voice raised, faith blazing in his chest, said without hesitation: "Just try to stop me."

It wasn't disrespectful—it was defiant in the best possible way. He wasn't about to let rules or protocol keep him from standing between heaven and earth on behalf of this little girl. We didn't know it yet, but grace was already at work. Mercy was moving in ways we couldn't see. And soon, we'd understand what it meant for those two to collide.

He walked up to me, threw his arms around me, and then embraced my wife. No words—just strength. Just presence. Then he stepped forward, into the hospital room, and gently laid his hand on our daughter's head. We gathered around. My wife and I stood beside him, barely able to breathe.

Then he began to pray. Not quiet, polite prayers. Not the kind of prayers you whisper at dinner. He prayed like life depended on it. Because it did.

He laid hands on her and prayed with boldness. With authority. With urgency. It wasn't emotionalism—it was faith rising up in a room that had felt like death just moments before. Scripture was spoken aloud. God's promises were declared. Tears fell. Hands trembled. Heaven was being called upon in a hospital room where we had run out of earthly options.

Just moments earlier, our little girl was sobbing in her hospital bed, her tiny body tense with pain and fear. But as we prayed over her, her cries began to soften. Her breathing steadied. Slowly, she relaxed, and then—like a miracle—she drifted into a peaceful sleep, her face calm for the first time in what felt like forever.

In that quiet, we knew God was there. I couldn't explain it then, and I still can't now. But the atmosphere changed. The weight that had been crushing my chest for hours began to lift. Hope crept in—not because the doctors had better news, but because God had entered the room. Not a dramatic voice from heaven. Not a miracle in that moment. But a deep, unmistakable sense that we were not alone. That the final word didn't belong to the doctors. That the diagnosis wasn't the end of the story. That our little girl was seen. Known. Held.

We didn't know what would happen next. We still didn't have answers. But for the first time that night, we had peace. And then . . . morning came. Our daughter was still with us.

After everything—after the warnings, the what-ifs, the long night of fear and whispered prayers—we woke up to the miracle we weren't sure we'd see. But that was only the beginning. Because then, her numbers started to change. Not all at once. Not in some movie-style, dramatic turnaround. But slowly. Steadily. As if the healing had already begun long before we even realized it.

The white blood cells that had vanished without explanation . . . started coming back. Bit by bit. Reading by reading. Hope was returning—in numbers, in breath, in the way the nurses started making eye contact again.

The doctors were baffled. They were cautious with their optimism. They double-checked the labs. They brought in more specialists. But in hushed tones, you could hear them circling the edge of something they didn't want to say. They were trying to explain what they could not explain. They danced around the word we already knew: *Miracle.*

This wasn't just medicine. This wasn't a lucky guess or the right antibiotic at the right time. This wasn't coincidence. This . . . was mercy. *"This I call to mind and therefore I have hope: The steadfast love of the Lord never ceases; his mercies never come to an end; they are new every morning; great is your faithfulness"* (Lamentations 3:21–23 ESV). I've never understood that verse more than I did in that moment. His mercy had come in the night . . . and His grace was waiting in the morning.

Our little girl, the one they told us might not make it, was still here. Still breathing. Still fighting. Still ours. And not because we earned it. Not because we prayed perfectly. But because of grace—unearned, undeserved, undeniable grace. *"By grace you have been saved, through faith—and this not of yourselves, it is the gift of God"* (Ephesians 2:8).

Looking back now, I can see it clearly. But at the time, I didn't fully understand what I was witnessing. I knew we had prayed. I knew we had trusted God, the best way we knew how. I had called in others who had more faith than me. I had done what I could.

But you know what I didn't have? I didn't have His Word. Not the kind that's written on paper. The kind that's written on your heart. I didn't have Scripture to stand on. I had phrases—things I'd heard other people say, promises passed around in church lobbies and waiting rooms. And I believed they were true, but I couldn't quote them. I couldn't cling to them. I didn't own them in the deep places of my soul.

When the panic hit, I didn't have the sword. *"Take . . . the sword of the Spirit, which is the word of God"* (Ephesians 6:17). And I've come to realize that you need it the most when the room goes quiet. When the hallway is cold. When the doctors are too quiet, and the machines are too loud. When you're desperate. When you're exhausted. When you're afraid that the next moment might be your last with the person you love most. That's when the Bible matters more than ever. Not because it gives you magic answers. But because it anchors you. *"Your word is a lamp to my feet and a light to my path"* (Psalm 119:105 ESV).

And when you're walking through the darkest night, you don't need a spotlight. You just need enough light to take the next step. God's Word is that light. I didn't have it in me that night. But I want to now. I want to be the kind of man who can say, "I trust You, Lord," and know what I'm standing on when I say it. *"The grass withers, the flower fades, but the word of our God stands forever"* (Isaiah 40:8 ESV).

That night taught me more than I could ever write in a journal. It taught me that God's grace shows up even when your faith feels fragile. His mercy doesn't wait until you've earned it. And that His Word—living, breathing, eternal—isn't optional. It's essential.

So, I don't read the Bible now because I feel like I should. I read it because I need it. Because someday, another crisis will come. Another diagnosis. Another long night. And when it does, I want more than prayers and panic. I want promises. I want truth I can hold onto like oxygen. Because I've seen what it feels like to stand in the middle of a miracle. And I never want to forget the God who gave it.

We left that hospital with joy. With praise. With gratitude, I didn't know how to express. I thanked God with everything I had in me. But here's the part that's hard to admit: I still didn't start reading His Word.

I had just witnessed a miracle—an undeniable move of God—and yet . . . I kept my Bible closed. I avoided the very thing meant to sustain me. I was grateful, emotional, changed—but not transformed.

And that's where grace comes in again. God didn't pull back. He didn't say, "You ungrateful son, after everything I've done?"

He didn't stop loving me because I didn't open my Bible the next morning. He didn't disqualify me for not running immediately into His Word. Instead, He waited. Patient. Kind. Still speaking, still guiding, still loving me—even as I ignored His most important invitation. That's grace.

*"But God demonstrates His own love for us in this: While we were still sinners, Christ died for us"* (Romans 5:8). That verse isn't just for your past; it's for your present—even when you're dodging Him, saying thanks but not staying, receiving the gift but ignoring the Giver's letter. God's grace was never about my performance or how fast I ran back to Him. It was about who He is. And He knew I wasn't ready yet. But He never stopped calling.

Looking back, I see it now: His miracle wasn't the end of the story; it was an invitation to begin a new one. I just didn't say yes . . . yet. And maybe, that's why this book had to be written. Not because I'm the most qualified, but because I'm honest about how I got it wrong. We learn from mistakes—ours and others. I just have plenty of both. And if my missteps can help someone else skip a few potholes on the road to grace, it's worth every scar.

You don't have to learn everything the hard way. You don't have to keep crashing into the same walls. Pick up your Bible—now. Not later. Not when you "feel more spiritual." Now. Throw away the excuses; they crumble under real need.

- Do you want to be better than you are right now?
- Do you want to be the best husband, wife, dad, mom, friend, or leader you can be?

If your answer is "Yes," pick up your Bible. If your answer is "No," reread Chapters 1 through 6. If your answer is "I'm already perfect," Congratulations. But you've probably wasted your time reading this book.

Here's the truth: Only God can make you the best version of yourself. And even when you think you've arrived, He will keep growing, shaping, and stretching you until the day you meet Him face to face. So, if you're tired of learning the hard way, pick up His Word:

- *"Your word is truth"* (John 17:17).
- *"They* [Your words] *are life to those who find them"* (Proverbs 4:22).
- "It shall not return . . . void" (Isaiah 55:11 KJV).

Everything you're searching for is already written. You just have to read it.

When we receive grace and mercy, that changes us because we know we don't deserve them. Grace and mercy soften our hearts, reshape our priorities, and show us what love looks like.

In the next chapter, we'll open God's Word and see grace and mercy in action: first, in the woman caught in adultery—standing in shame yet forgiven by Jesus; then, in the thief on the cross—who found paradise through desperate faith in his final moments.

These stories remind us that grace isn't just a nice idea—it's God's heart poured out on real people with real failures, and it's the same grace offered to you and me today. Let's step into these moments together and let their beauty sink deep.

# Chapter 13:

# GRACE UPON GRACE

*Grace is God giving us what we could never earn—and what we least deserve.*

## A Woman Caught in Adultery – The Story

Early in the morning, Jesus arrived at the temple courts. Crowds gathered around Him, eager for His words. But before He could teach, a commotion erupted—angry voices, scuffling feet, and a woman's sobs. The religious leaders stormed into the courtyard, dragging a terrified woman. Her hair tangled, her eyes red and puffy, her body trembling with each step. They shoved her into the center of the crowd, right at Jesus's feet.

"*Teacher,*" they said, almost spitting the word, "*this woman was caught in the act of adultery. In the Law Moses commanded us to stone such women. Now what do you say*" (John 8:4–5)? This was no search for justice; it was a trap, a cruel game to corner Jesus. The woman could barely lift her head. Her heart pounded in terror. Death felt certain. Her breath came in ragged gasps as she waited for the first stone to fly. Her mind must have spiraled: How did it come to this? Does God see me now only in my shame?

Jesus bent down and wrote on the ground with His finger. The world seemed to slow around her. The crowd grew quiet; the accusers leaned forward, waiting. What was He writing? Each heartbeat thundered in her chest. They pressed Him again for an answer. Jesus straightened, His eyes steady and searching theirs—and perhaps brushing over hers with piercing compassion—and He declared: "*Let any one of you who is without sin be the first to throw a stone at her.*" (John 8:7).

He stooped again, resuming His writing in the dust. Time felt suspended. The woman closed her eyes, bracing for the pain she was sure would follow. But instead, there was silence. Then a dull thud—one stone fell to the ground. Another. And another. Footsteps retreated. One by one, the accusers left, oldest to youngest, each convicted by their own guilt.

At last, she dared to look up. The courtyard was empty except for Jesus. His gaze met hers—not with condemnation but with kindness deeper than she could fathom. His voice was gentle, yet powerful enough to scatter every shame-filled lie she believed: "*Woman, where are they? Has no one condemned you*" (John 8:10)?

Tears streamed down her face as relief and gratitude overwhelmed her. "*No one, sir,*" she whispered, breathless with disbelief. Jesus spoke words that must have melted every fear and filled her with life: "*Then neither do I condemn you. . . . Go now and leave your life of sin*" (John 8:11).

In that moment, her heart must have exploded with thankfulness—this man had saved her life, seen her shame, and offered hope when she deserved none. She had come expecting death, but she left with forgiveness, a new future, and a deeper love for God than she had ever known.

This isn't just a story about judgment avoided; it's a breathtaking moment of mercy and gratitude, showing how Jesus meets us in our deepest shame with a forgiveness that calls us into freedom.

## What Can We Learn from the Woman Caught in Adultery?

The story of the woman caught in adultery (John 8:1–11) is one of the most raw and redemptive moments in all of Scripture. She was caught in the act—humiliated, exposed, and dragged into the temple courts like a trophy of shame. Her accusers didn't care about justice or her soul—they were using her brokenness to trap Jesus. She stood there surrounded by stones and judgment, not just from the crowd but likely from herself. In her mind, it was over. She had sinned. She was guilty. And now, she was alone. Or so she thought.

Then Jesus stooped. Not to throw a stone—but to write in the dirt. We don't know what He wrote, but we know what He said: "*Let any one of you who is without sin be the first to throw a stone.*" With that sentence, Jesus flipped the courtroom. The accusers became the accused. Stones began to fall, not in violence, but in surrender. And when it was quiet—when her heart was still racing and her tears were still fresh—Jesus looked at her with a gaze that didn't flinch. "*Woman, where are they* [your accusers]?" He asked. "*Has no one condemned you?*" When she said, "*No one,*" He responded with words that still change lives today: "*Then neither do I condemn you. Go and sin no more.*"

From this story, we learn that Jesus doesn't sweep sin under the rug, but He does kneel in the dirt to meet us in it. He doesn't justify our mistakes, but He refuses to let them define us. Grace doesn't ignore the truth; it just adds love to it. This woman deserved judgment. She got Jesus instead. And that's what we all need. He didn't minimize her sin, but He also didn't maximize her shame. He gave her something far more powerful than punishment: a second chance.

This story also teaches us something about ourselves: We're quick to pick up stones. Maybe not literal ones—but the kind we throw with our words, our judgments, our social media posts, or our silent comparisons. But if Jesus—who was without sin—chose not to condemn, what right do we have to do otherwise? Grace calls us to drop our stones, check our hearts, and remember that we're all just one bad decision away from being the woman in the circle.

And finally, we learn that Jesus meets us in our lowest moment and still sees a future. His *"go and sin no more"* wasn't a guilt trip—it was an invitation to freedom. He was saying, "You don't have to stay in this story. You're not stuck in your shame. You're free now—so live like it."

That's the power of grace. That's the mercy of Jesus. And that's the hope for all of us who have ever stood in the circle of our worst mistakes, thinking it was over—only to hear the voice of the Savior saying, "I'm not done with you yet."

## Beside the Savior, a Thief – The Story

*I deserved death, but beside Jesus, I found a hope stronger than my failures.*

The hill of Golgotha was a scene of horror: three crosses silhouetted against a sky growing dark at midday. Roman soldiers stood guard, religious leaders sneered, and a restless crowd watched the spectacle unfold. In the center, Jesus hung bruised and bloodied—His face unrecognizable; His breaths ragged. On either side of Him, two criminals hung dying.

One thief could see nothing beyond his own pain. Spitting curses, he sneered: *"Aren't you the Messiah? Save yourself and us"* (Luke 23:39)! His words dripped with rage, wanting rescue without repentance, salvation without surrender.

But the other thief watched Jesus closely. Even as he himself gasped for breath, every tortured rise and fall of his chest brought new clarity. He saw the sign above Jesus's head declaring, "King of the Jews." He heard Jesus's words of compassion for those who nailed Him there: "*Father, forgive them, for they do not know what they are doing*" (Luke 23:34). He noticed Jesus's calm authority despite His agony. Slowly, it dawned on him: This man isn't like us. He's innocent. He's righteous. He is exactly who He claims to be.

Every memory of violence and selfishness in his own life came crashing down. His crimes weren't mere mistakes—they were rebellion. And yet, right next to him was a man who looked heavenward, not with hatred, but with love. A king. Breaking through his pain, he rebuked the other criminal: "*Don't you fear God*," he gasped, "*since you are under the same sentence? We are punished justly, for we are getting what our deeds deserve. But this man has done nothing wrong*" (Luke 23:40–41).

That confession was monumental. In a moment of raw honesty, he acknowledged his guilt and Jesus's innocence, publicly proclaiming Jesus's righteousness from a cross. Then, with every ounce of strength left, he turned his head, met Jesus's eyes, and cried out words that must have been filled with trembling hope: "*Jesus, remember me when you come into your kingdom*" (Luke 23:42).

It was a prayer of desperate faith: I believe you are King. I believe you have a kingdom beyond death. I believe you can save even me. Jesus, beaten and crowned with thorns, looked back with compassion blazing brighter than the sun that now hid its face. His words shattered the despair of the thief's final hours: "*Truly I tell you, today you will be with me in paradise*" (Luke 23:43).

The man's body still hung dying, but his soul leapt alive. Peace must have flooded him in that moment—a peace he had never known, a peace that no one could steal. His last breaths were not spent cursing fate, but resting in the promise of the King beside him. He died forgiven, free, and forever changed—because even on the cross, Jesus came to seek and save the lost.

## What Can We Learn from the Thief?

The story of the thief on the cross teaches us that true faith begins the moment we stop pretending we're innocent and finally recognize our need for a Savior. His life was marked by failure, rebellion, and regret—yet in his final breath, he found grace. That's the heart of the gospel: Even a life littered with sin isn't beyond God's reach.

God's intention in that moment wasn't just to comfort one dying man, but to declare something eternal: His mercy has no limits. By offering paradise to a condemned criminal—someone with no opportunity to clean up his act or earn forgiveness—Jesus showed the world that grace is a gift, not a reward. The thief's plea, *"Remember me,"* wasn't eloquent or polished. It was desperate, honest, and enough.

What we can take away is simple yet life-changing: Jesus responds instantly to sincere faith. No delay. No checklist. Just grace. His promise of paradise was stronger than the thief's worst regrets—and that same promise is offered to us the moment we turn to Him.

This story remains profoundly relevant because so many people believe they've missed their chance with God. But Jesus's words remind us: It's never too late, and you're never too far gone. One honest cry for mercy is all it takes to move from death to eternal life.

Ultimately, this story shows us who we are—sinners in need of saving—and reveals who Jesus is: the innocent King who bore our punishment and freely offers salvation to all who believe. It captures the essence of the gospel and the mission of Christ: *"to seek and save the lost"* (Luke 19:10). It reminds us that God's kingdom isn't earned by good behavior or long devotion, but it is entered by grace through faith, even in our final moments.

# Chapter 14:
# FROM WOUNDED TO WHOLE

*Even in our darkest chapters, God's love can write a new ending—because hope always remains.*

I almost left this chapter out. Not because I didn't think it would help someone, but because including it means exposing something I've spent a lifetime trying to keep hidden. Writing it means opening a door I've kept locked. And once it's open, it's open for good.

Telling this part of my story leaves me vulnerable. It's a story told from a place of forgiveness; even so . . . a heart that's been broken—even one that's been healed—still shows scars. And the truth is, some scars come from wounds so deep, so personal, so out-of-order that they don't just hurt, they rearrange you. They disrupt things you didn't even know could be touched. They steal things before you've had the chance to know what they were.

That's what abuse does. It doesn't just take something from a child in the moment. It takes what that child was supposed to give to others later. It reaches into the future; it's a theft that keeps on stealing. The loss isn't just physical. It's emotional, spiritual, and relational. It's the loss of how you were supposed to love, connect, trust, express, receive, and offer comfort. You may grow up thinking you're okay, but something's missing. You can say, "I love you," but it might not feel like love on the inside. You can show up for others but not know how to let them show up for you. You can protect your kids fiercely, and still not know how to let them feel emotionally safe with you.

That's because what was taken . . . wasn't just innocence. It was the ability to be open, to be tender, and to feel safe in your own skin. And when you don't know what's missing, you don't know how to pass it on. So yes, I've forgiven the one who took from me what wasn't theirs to take. But the echo of that wound didn't stop with me. It followed me into marriage, into fatherhood, and into my faith.

I became a man who could show strength, but struggled to show softness. I knew how to protect but not how to be present. I could provide but not always connect. That's the part I still grieve—not for myself but for my wife and daughters. The anger that lingers isn't toward the past anymore; it's toward the parts of me I couldn't give them.

John 10:10 says, "*The thief comes only to steal and kill and destroy.*" I lived a long time in the shadow of that verse. But thank God, that's not where the story ends. Jesus continues, "*I came that they may have life, and have it abundantly*" (John 10:10 ESV).

This is not a story of destruction. This is a story of redemption. Yes, what happened changed me. Yes, scars remain. But so does grace because God has been rewriting what the enemy tried to erase. The healing wasn't instant; it wasn't pretty; it didn't follow a formula. But it came. And the miracle? I'm still becoming the man I never got to see growing up. Not because I figured it out. But because I finally gave God the broken pieces, and He didn't throw any of them away. "*He heals the brokenhearted and binds up their wounds*" (Psalm 147:30).

So, I share this chapter not to reopen the wound, but to tell the truth. To tell you what was lost—and who gave me the strength to start giving again. To remind you that scars don't disqualify you. They're evidence that healing happened. And that even this—even this can be used for good.

Forgiveness isn't a feeling—it's a process. And it doesn't begin when the pain goes away; it begins when you decide the pain can't be the one calling the shots anymore. With something as personal and devastating as sexual abuse, forgiveness can feel like betrayal—like you're letting someone off the hook. But that's not what forgiveness is. It's not saying what happened was okay. It's saying, "I won't let what they did define who I am."

You don't have to wait until the memory fades or the emotions stop crashing into you. Begin where you are—with trembling hands and a soul that wants freedom more than revenge. But here's the truth I had to wrestle with: You can't fully forgive until you stop blaming yourself. That's where the real war starts. It's not just against the person who hurt you—it's against the lies you've carried ever since. The lie that says, "Maybe I did something to deserve it." The whisper that says, "Maybe I let it happen." Those thoughts are cruel, but they come, especially in silence.

Part of the forgiveness process is learning to speak truth to yourself: "I didn't cause this. I didn't invite this. I was a child. And what was done to me was wrong." Before I could ever offer forgiveness to someone else, I had to stop punishing myself for something I didn't do. That's why I want you to know this before I tell my story: Forgiveness had to come first. Not because I'm strong, but because anger can't be the narrator. Hurt can't be the one holding the pen. If I had tried to write this from the place where I started—from shame, confusion, and fury—I would've told a very different story.

But healing has a way of softening what once burned. Forgiveness didn't erase the memory, but it gave me back my voice. And now, I can tell the truth—not to get even, not to get pity—but to give hope. Because if you've ever felt what I felt, I need you to know: Freedom is possible.

When you grow up with a stepdad who's always drunk and resents you because you're not his, it leaves a mark. To him, I wasn't a kid who needed love. I was just a reminder of someone else. A bill he didn't sign up for.

And let me pause right here and say something important: I know not every stepfather is like that. I know there are incredible men out there—men who step into broken homes and become whole-hearted fathers to children who aren't biologically theirs and love those kids as their own. Those who show up, stay, and give more than what's asked of them. Some of the best dads I've ever seen weren't the ones who shared DNA—they were the ones who showed up when they didn't have to. But that just wasn't my story.

In my case, my stepdad's attention was something to avoid. He was angry. Unpredictable. His version of "fathering" came with raised voices, slurred words, and the kind of fear that teaches a kid to stay quiet and stay out of the way. His greatest contribution to my life was motivating me to leave as soon as I was old enough to walk out the door.

And my biological dad? In my opinion, a deadbeat. He never took responsibility—not for me, not for his words, not for anything. His mouth was his weapon of choice. He didn't just speak cruelly— he seemed to enjoy it. Like, hurting people made him feel powerful.

So, getting attention from the men in my life was never something I longed for. I didn't crave it; I learned to survive without it. Which is why, when a man came into my life later and actually saw me—and not just saw me, but said things like, "You'd be any dad's dream," it was disorienting.

When someone shows up and says the kind of words you always wanted to hear, wants to spend time with you, teach you, invest in you, it's hard not to be drawn to that. Especially when you've never had it. This man was never a threat to me, at least not at first. He never said anything inappropriate. He never made me feel uncomfortable. He was funny, reassuring, and seemed to genuinely care. I remember thinking, this guy should have kids. He'd be a great dad.

He knew everything—or at least it felt that way to a twelve-year-old boy who had never had a steady male figure to look up to. And the best part? He wanted to teach me. He saw how much I loved cars and leaned into it. He showed me how engines worked. How to use tools. How to clean a windshield without leaving streaks. He explained little things like body lines, paint depth, and chrome trim. No fishing. No backyard football. No lectures. Just time, interest, and the kind of steady attention I'd always longed for.

That's what made it so easy to trust him. Being with him felt like what I thought spending time with a real dad must be like—comfortable, safe, and steady. The day the *Cars of the Stars* museum opened in Southern California, I snuck in. I couldn't help it—I was obsessed with cars. They had everything: TV icons, movie legends, even The Beatles' Bentley. I got caught, of course—but instead of kicking me out, the owner offered me a job. I was stunned. After school, I'd sweep floors, dust cars, and straighten brochures like it was the best job in the world. That's where I met him—the man with the connections. He noticed my passion, took me under his wing, and started bringing me along to deliver cars to the studios.

And since I was too young to drive, and home wasn't exactly a place where people tracked where I was going, no one thought twice when I said, "I'm going with him." My mom would nod and wave me off. No questions. No hesitation.

I don't think it was neglect out of cruelty—just distraction. Chaos makes anything that looks calm seem safe. And looking back, maybe that's why no one saw it coming. Why no one ever thought to ask if I was okay. I'll do my best to just say it.

One day, I asked my mom if I could go with him to his house overnight. He lived in Hollywood, and he said he wanted to introduce me to an actor from *The Waltons* TV show. Just to be clear, that actor was kind, respectful, and friendly. I only mention it because it was part of what made the whole thing feel legitimate. Real. Exciting. Safe.

And when I asked, my mom said yes. I was twelve years old. I had never been to this man's house, and barely anyone in my family knew anything about him. But like always, she just said, "Be careful." That was her default parenting advice. *Be careful.* So, I went.

And honestly? At first, it was incredible. I met a few actors. We talked. We laughed. It was fun. He really knew these people. He didn't just tell stories—he had connections, photos, proof. And I couldn't believe someone like that thought so much of me. He acted like I mattered. Like I was worth his time. I didn't question why. I didn't care why. Because around him, I felt normal. More than that—I felt wanted.

He taught me things. Bragged about how quickly I picked up on them. I told him once about this story my mom always shared when I was little—the one that made me feel like something was wrong with me. As I mentioned earlier, no one ever corrected that narrative. No one ever told me, "That story isn't who you are." But I guess I was wrong. Because he did. He was the first one to say, "That doesn't make you broken. You're smart. You're okay." And I can't even explain what that meant to me.

It's hard to say this next part. Hard because it sounds so twisted now, but at the time, it felt pure. I started to believe he loved me—

not in a weird way, but in the way a dad might love a son. Like I was the kid he never had. I cringe even writing that, but it's the truth. And if you think I haven't deleted this chapter over and over again, trying to escape the shame of that thought, you'd be wrong. I've rewritten it more times than I can count. I've wanted to leave it out. But I can't.

Because the truth is, I was that kid. That naïve, hopeful, vulnerable kid who believed someone had finally chosen him for the right reasons. Who thought someone saw value in him without strings attached. But people don't usually invest without expecting a return. And I carried that realization for years. Decades. Honestly, even now—writing this—I still feel some of its weight.

I won't share details. But I will tell you this: That night, I didn't get to go home. I wanted to—more than I'd ever wanted anything in my life. And that says a lot, considering the kind of home I had. Dysfunctional. Loud. Sometimes violent. But that night, I would've given anything just to be back there.

Because the truth had finally surfaced. It was all a lie. He never cared. Not really. He groomed me. He saw what I longed for and handed me a counterfeit version of it. He gave me the kind of affection I'd been desperate for, the kind of attention I thought I'd never have. He made me believe I was something—*something*. And I believed it.

I felt like a fool. But I wouldn't be fooled again. I'm not telling this story to get sympathy. I'm not using it as an excuse for my flaws or failures. I'm telling it because this chapter is about forgiveness, and if I'm going to be honest about what it means, I have to show you what it costs.

I carried this pain for most of my life. I buried it, locked it away, and tried to live above it. But when I accepted Christ as a teenager and heard the pastor talk about God as our "heavenly

Father," I flinched inside. *Father?* That word didn't bring comfort. It brought confusion and anger. Silence. Where were you, God? I carried that question with me, right into adulthood. Right into my marriage. It wasn't until years later that I finally told my wife. I shared the story slowly and with fear. I was sure she'd look at me differently. But she didn't. She cried. She loved me. She held me. And for the first time in my life, I felt something that looked like freedom. Not total healing, but the beginning of it. Because speaking the truth out loud—finally giving it a name—took away some of its power.

Her response taught me something about the love of the real Father. The kind I didn't grow up with, but was learning to trust. But the wound followed me into fatherhood, too. It showed up in ways I never expected. I loved my daughters deeply, but I struggled with closeness. Something in me was afraid—afraid that if I kissed them too much, held them too long, tickled them like normal dads do, they'd wonder, *Why is Daddy doing that?* I knew it was a lie, but the fear was loud. So, I pulled back. I held back.

And it broke me. Because that's what a predator takes. Not just from the one they abuse, but from everyone that child will one day try to love. That's the ripple effect. It's not just pain—it's stolen joy, stolen closeness, stolen confidence in the goodness of love. And that's why forgiveness matters. Because without it, the wound keeps stealing.

Carrying unforgiveness is like dragging a heavy chain behind you. Sometimes, you forget it's there, but it's always slowing you down. It wears on your heart. It hardens your perspective. It colors how you see the world and how you see yourself. At first, it feels like protection—like holding onto anger will keep you from ever being hurt again. But in reality, unforgiveness doesn't shield us; it cages us.

Jesus didn't downplay the pain people cause. He was betrayed, abandoned, and crucified by those He came to save. Yet from the cross, He said, "*Father, forgive them*" (Luke 23:34). Not because they deserved it. But because that's who He is.

And when we withhold forgiveness, we step outside of the grace we've been given. The Bible is clear—forgiveness is not optional. It is foundational. In Ephesians 4:32, we're told to "*be kind and compassionate to one another, forgiving each other, just as in Christ God forgave you.*" That means forgiveness doesn't start with the other person. It starts with remembering how much we've been forgiven.

Forgiveness isn't saying what the offender did was okay—it's saying *I won't let that control me anymore.* We forgive not because someone deserves it, but because God has already shown us mercy we didn't deserve. That's the model. That's the standard. And it's hard, especially when the wound is deep and the damage is lasting. But Jesus never asked us to do it alone. He said, "*With man this is impossible, but with God all things are possible*" (Matthew 19:26).

And here's what often surprises people: The healing comes after the forgiveness, not before. You won't feel completely ready to forgive. You may not feel peace at first. But when you choose to forgive—even in weakness—you open the door for healing to begin. You free yourself from the grip of bitterness. You release the other person, yes, but more importantly, you release yourself.

That's when the burden lifts. That's when the scars stop burning and start softening.

Forgiveness isn't forgetting. It's remembering with grace instead of rage. It's choosing freedom. And when you walk in that freedom, you begin to live the life God always meant for you, not defined by the past, but redeemed through it. Here's the hardest part about telling stories like this: You never really know how it will land.

You write with trembling hands, not knowing if the words will be received as a cry for help, a declaration of freedom, or something in between. Vulnerability isn't tidy—it's raw. It's risky. You hand over your scars and just pray they aren't mishandled. You wonder if people will still see you the same, or if the honesty will shift something in their eyes. It's not just about being judged. It's about being misunderstood. About someone taking your surrender and mislabeling it as weakness—or worse, seeing your pain and calling it attention-seeking.

But if we only ever show the polished versions of our stories—the Instagram-filtered faith, the highlight reel of healing—we rob others of the real hope that comes from messy, in-progress, still-bleeding redemption. So, I'm sharing mine.

Not for sympathy. Not for shock. But because I believe someone reading this is sitting where I once sat—ashamed of what they've survived and afraid of what healing might cost. This wasn't easy to write. And if it wasn't easy to read, that's okay. That means we're being honest. That means we're getting somewhere real. Just don't stop here.

Because freedom—the kind that changes everything—is on the other side of the truth you're terrified to say out loud. And when you're ready to say it . . . God will be right there. Not to judge but to hold it with you, to walk you through it, and to turn even this into a story worth telling. Now, it's time to leave this chapter in the rearview mirror because God's Word shows us, we're not the first to know deep pain, and we're not alone in our struggle.

Next, we'll step into the stories of Tamar, who bore the agony of sexual assault, and Job, who faced a storm of loss and grief. These ancient stories don't just echo our pain; they reveal a God who meets us in it, stays with us through it, and promises redemption beyond what we can see now. Let's turn the page together and discover how God brings light into even the darkest places.

# Chapter 15:
# WHEN PAIN HAS NO WORDS

*Tamar's courage turned disgrace into destiny. When others wrote her off, God wrote her in—proving that even in the darkest chapters, His redemption is still unfolding.*

## Tamar's Assault – The Story

Her innocence was stolen, her voice silenced, and her heart left shattered in a world that looked away. Tamar was a princess of Israel—King David's daughter—and the younger sister of Absalom, one of the most powerful and handsome men in the kingdom. But despite her royal status and her father's power, Tamar was vulnerable in a way that no title could protect.

Her half-brother Amnon, David's eldest son and heir to the throne, became obsessed with her. His desire wasn't love; it was selfish, consuming lust. Day after day, he fixated on her beauty until he became physically sick. But instead of repenting or confessing his struggle, he allowed it to fester.

Amnon's cousin Jonadab, known for being "a very shrewd man," noticed his growing misery and asked him what was wrong. Amnon confided in Jonadab about his twisted craving. Rather than warn

Amnon or tell David, Jonadab devised a scheme: Pretend to be ill and when your father visits, ask him to send Tamar to cook for you so you can be alone with her.

King David, perhaps worried about his son's apparent illness, agreed. When Tamar was called, she came innocently, bringing warmth and kindness. She prepared bread in front of Amnon, kneading the dough, baking it, and bringing it to his bedside—her every move motivated by compassion, completely unaware of the darkness about to unfold.

As she handed him the bread, Amnon ordered everyone else out of the room. Suddenly, the silence of the empty chamber turned sinister. The kindness in his eyes twisted into hunger. He grabbed Tamar and demanded: "*Come to bed with me, my sister*" (2 Samuel 13:11).

Terror filled Tamar's heart. She pleaded, her voice breaking: "*No, my brother! . . . Don't force me! Such a thing should not be done in Israel! Don't do this wicked thing*" (2 Samuel 13:12). She offered a desperate compromise, begging him to speak to the king—even though the Law prohibited their union—just to delay the unthinkable. But Amnon wouldn't listen. Overpowered by his lust, he forced her down and raped her, crushing her innocence and shattering her dignity.

What happened next was even more heartbreaking: "*Then Amnon hated her with intense hatred. . . . He hated her more than he had loved her*" (2 Samuel 13:15). The girl he couldn't live without became the object of his scorn. He barked cruelly: "*Get up and get out*" (2 Samuel 13:15).

Tamar's voice, trembling and desperate, rose once more: "*No!*" she cried. "*Sending me away would be a greater wrong than what you have already done to me*" (2 Samuel 13:16). But Amnon wouldn't hear it. He called his servant, ordering: "*Get this woman out of my sight and bolt the door after her*" (2 Samuel 13:17), reducing his sister—his victim—to a nameless object: "*this woman.*"

Thrown out like trash, Tamar tore her ornate robe, the symbol of her royal virginity and honor, poured ashes on her head, and wept aloud as she ran. Her tears were more than grief—they were the sound of a soul crushed by betrayal. She fled to the house of her brother Absalom. Seeing her torn robe and tear-streaked face, Absalom asked: *"Has that Amnon, your brother, been with you"* (2 Samuel 13:20)? His words hinted at what everyone feared—and Tamar must have felt utterly exposed, ashamed, and alone.

Then Absalom's response landed like another blow: "Be quiet now, my sister; he is your brother. Don't take this thing to heart." Whether meant to protect her from more harm or to avoid scandal, his words told Tamar to bury her trauma.

The text records the tragic outcome of her life: *"And Tamar lived in her brother Absalom's house, a desolate woman"* (2 Samuel 13:20). Her world had been reduced to silence and shame. Meanwhile, King David heard of all this and was furious, but he did nothing. His passivity allowed the wound to fester, not only in Tamar's heart but in his family. Absalom's rage grew until, two years later, he took vengeance into his own hands, murdering Amnon. This act would ignite a chain of events that tore David's family apart, leading to rebellion, death, and heartbreak.

This isn't just a story of one woman's assault; it's a brutal window into the reality of abuse, betrayal, and the deep, unhealed wounds victims can carry.

## What Can We Learn from Tamar's Story?

Tamar's story teaches us that God's Word doesn't hide the reality of abuse—it exposes it. Her suffering reveals what happens when those with power choose silence over justice and self over protection. It shows us that God is not blind to injustice. He sees the oppressed, grieves with the brokenhearted, and refuses to erase their pain from His story.

God's intention in including Tamar's story was to make sure her voice—and the voices of all victims—would not be forgotten. It reminds us that abuse is never the victim's fault. God's heart burns against injustice, and His presence enters even the most shattered places to bring healing.

This story is painfully relevant today. Abuse still hides behind silence; shame still isolates; and too many still look away. Tamar's cry calls us to speak up, stand up, and be the kind of people who protect and restore. Ultimately, this story tells us who we are: people living in a broken world where injustice is real, but also people seen, loved, and fiercely defended by a God who promises to bring justice and heal every wound.

Tamar's heartbreak points forward to the healing Jesus came to bring. Her lonely cry becomes part of the gospel echo—one that reminds us that God sent His Son to bind up the brokenhearted and that He will one day right every wrong.

Tamar's pain came from people; Job's came from circumstances. One was betrayal; the other was mystery. But both asked the same question: Where is God when it hurts this much? Whether wounds are caused by injustice or loss, God is still near, and even when we have no words, He hears every cry.

## Job Restored- The Story

*Though the world crumbles and answers never come, faith whispers: my Redeemer lives.*

In the quiet, sunbaked land of Uz, Job's life overflowed with blessings. He had ten children—seven sons and three daughters—who loved to gather and feast together, celebrating life in a harmony that would even be rare among families today. His wealth was staggering: Thousands of sheep, camels, oxen, and donkeys grazed and labored across his fields. Servants bustled around his household, and his name commanded respect in every village and city. But more than all that, Job's character was unmatched: He *"was blameless and upright; he feared God and shunned evil"* (Job 1:1).

Every morning, Job rose early to offer sacrifices for his children, just in case they had sinned in their hearts during their feasting. His love wasn't casual; it was a fierce, protective devotion. He carried a heart burdened with reverence, constantly interceding for his family.

Yet even as Job lived a life of integrity, a cosmic conversation unfolded in heaven. The angels came before God, and with them came Satan, the accuser. God pointed to Job with divine pride: *"Have you considered my servant Job? There is no one on earth like him"* (Job 1:8). But Satan sneered: Of course Job fears you— You've built a hedge around him! Take it all away, and he'll curse you to Your face. So, God gave Satan permission to test Job, but not to touch his body.

One seemingly normal day, everything changed forever. A servant burst into Job's courtyard, breathless, dirt on his clothes: He reported that the Sabeans had attacked and stolen the oxen and donkeys and killed Job's servants. Before that servant finished speaking, another arrived: *"The fire of God fell from heavens and burned up the sheep and the servants and consumed them"* (Job 1:16 ESV). Then a third servant stumbled in: "The Chaldeans formed raiding parties—your camels are gone, and the servants are dead!" Job's mind must have spun, each blow harder to process than the last.

But nothing could prepare him for the final messenger: "Your sons and daughters were feasting when a mighty wind struck the house—it collapsed, and they are all dead." Every parent's worst nightmare descended. His children—the joy of his heart—were gone in an instant. Ten precious lives extinguished.

Job's response was astonishing: He tore his robe, shaved his head in raw grief, and fell face down to the ground—not to curse, but to worship: *"Naked I came from my mother's womb, and naked I will depart. The Lord gave and the Lord has taken away; may the name of the Lord be praised"* (Job 1:21).

But Satan wasn't finished. He returned to heaven, certain that Job's faith would break if his body were afflicted. God allowed it, forbidding only Job's death. Painful boils erupted across Job's skin—from head to toe, open sores that oozed, stank, and refused to heal. In agony, Job sat on an ash heap, scraping his wounds with a broken piece of pottery, the most powerful man in the East reduced to a pitiful shadow of himself.

His wife, equally crushed but drowning in bitterness, spoke the unthinkable: *"Are you still maintaining your integrity? Curse God and die"* (Job 2:9)! Her words must have cut deeper than any physical wound—how lonely Job must have felt in that moment. But he replied with quiet strength: *"Shall we accept good from God, and not trouble"* (Job 2:10)?

Job's friends—Eliphaz, Bildad, and Zophar—arrived and sat with him for seven days and nights, stunned by his suffering. They wept and tore their robes, unable to speak. But when they finally opened their mouths, their words stung. Instead of comfort, they accused: You must have sinned, Job; God wouldn't punish a righteous man. Their accusations grew sharper with each round of speeches, adding insult to Job's unimaginable injuries. They insisted God was fair, so Job's suffering had to be his fault. But Job knew he had not done evil to deserve this, and their false counsel deepened his anguish.

In his laments, Job poured out his pain with searing honesty: *"Why did I not perish at birth"* (Job 3:11)? *"Why is light given to those in misery, and life to the bitter of soul"* (Job 3:20)? He raged, wept, and pleaded for answers. His friends' theology couldn't explain his pain, and God seemed silent.

As days stretched into weeks, Job's suffering felt endless. The sores, the stares of his neighbors, the sting of his wife's words, the relentless condemnation from friends—all compounded the devastation of losing his children. Job felt abandoned, even cursed. Yet again and again, he returned to his conviction: "*Though he slay me, yet will I hope in him*" (Job 13:15).

Though Job's story spans forty-two chapters, the opening scenes alone capture a soul-crushing agony few can fathom. They show a man stripped of everything—wealth, health, reputation, and family—and yet clinging, sometimes by a thread, to a God he couldn't understand.

This isn't just a story of loss; it's a raw, honest portrayal of what it means to worship through weeping and trust when nothing makes sense. So, what can we learn from Job's anguish? What was God's intention? What can we take away, and why does this story still matter today? Let's unpack it.

## What Can We Learn from This Story and Job?

Job's story pulls back the curtain on one of life's most difficult questions: Why do the righteous suffer? It doesn't give us all the answers, but it gives us something far more powerful. It gives us a God who is present in the silence, faithful in the mystery, and still worthy of worship when life falls apart.

We learn that faith isn't about having everything figured out. It's about choosing to hold on when nothing makes sense. Job didn't pretend to be okay. He poured out his anguish in unfiltered laments. He argued, grieved, questioned, and cried out—not with rebellion, but with reverent honesty. His story shows us that God can handle our pain. He invites it. And He meets us in it.

God's intention wasn't to test Job for sport or to punish him. It was to show the world what real devotion looks like—not rooted in blessings or ease, but in love. Job loved God not for what He gave, but for who He was. In allowing Job's faith to be refined through suffering, God proved that righteousness isn't something we fake or earn—it's something forged in fire.

This story speaks to our generation more than ever. We live in a world where tragedy strikes without warning—diagnoses, losses, betrayals, financial collapse. And when it does, the question that haunts us isn't always why; sometimes, our most pressing question is, "Where is God in this?" Job answers with conviction: "*Though He slay me, yet will I hope in Him.*" That kind of hope is costly. It's honest. And it's holy.

We learn that even when God seems silent, He is never absent. And when the people closest to us—like Job's wife and friends—offer more hurt than healing, God remains steady. He sees every tear, counts every sigh, and honors every flicker of faith we dare to lift in the darkness.

Ultimately, Job's story is our story. We are people who suffer and don't always get the answers we want. But we're also people made in the image of a God who entered our suffering, bore our sorrows, and promises to restore all that was lost. Job's cries echo in Jesus's voice at the cross—"*My God, my God, why have you forsaken me*" (Matthew 27:46). But so does his hope—because the redeemer that Job longed for is the very Christ who came to conquer sin and death, promising that our suffering will never be the end of the story. Because the same God who allowed Job's testing sent His Son to redeem every ounce of pain we will ever endure.

And just as Job was restored—not with the same children, but with a renewed life, deeper faith, and multiplied blessing—our hope is not just for comfort in this life, but for the day when "*He will wipe every tear from their eyes. There will be no more death or mourning or crying or pain"* (Revelation 21:4).

So, what does this mean for us today? It means our pain isn't wasted. Our questions aren't disqualifying. Our endurance matters. And our Redeemer lives. Because of Jesus, even the hardest chapters aren't the end of the story; they're the ground where glory begins to grow.

# Chapter 16:
# THE POWER OF SURRENDER

*When we let go of control, open hands become the place where God places His best gifts.*

Before we go any further, we need to stop and sit with something that's been woven into every chapter so far. I've hinted at it, maybe grazed it with emotion. But now it's time to name it: surrender. In this chapter, we will reflect on what it is, why it matters, and how it connects to everything we've talked about: our excuses, avoidance, confusion, and struggle to open the Bible in the first place.

This chapter isn't just another stop—it's a turning point. Because without surrender, your walk with God might always feel off. Like you're spiritually limping and don't know why. Let's start with the obvious: Surrender is hard. It sounds good in a worship song, but in real life, it's terrifying. And if we're honest, most of us don't know what it looks like. We think it's giving up a few bad habits, maybe ditching a toxic relationship or trading a beach vacation for a mission trip.

But surrender isn't a single moment—it's a lifestyle. Surrender is a posture that says, "God, I'm not just giving You what I don't like—I'm giving You what I still want to control." And that's where things get real because control is usually the last thing we want to give up. Especially when we've spent years—maybe decades—building a life that makes us feel safe or successful.

If you're anything like me, you didn't stumble into control—you planned it. I color-coded my life. Career. Finances. Even my spirituality. I had Jesus close enough to feel safe, but not close enough to make changes. Like a spiritual seatbelt—you hope you never need it, but it's nice to have. Here's what I learned: As long as I was in control, I couldn't be transformed.

The Bible didn't start to come alive for me until I came to it with empty hands—when I stopped trying to edit my story and started asking God to rewrite it. That's why surrender isn't just an idea in this book; it's the answer to all the questions we've been asking:

- Why do we make excuses not to read the Bible? Because it threatens our control.
- Why do we avoid it? Because surrender is uncomfortable.
- Why does it feel confusing? Because we come to it on our terms, not God's.

But when you finally surrender, Scripture stops being confusing and becomes convicting. And conviction leads to change. At first, I stumbled through surrender. My hands were full—plans, pride, performance. But I kept convincing myself I was making progress. Eventually, God stopped letting me trip. He pulled the rug. Hard. And I fell. No more pretending. No more curated plans. Just me, face down, out of options.

That's when it hit me: Surrender wasn't one option. It was the only way forward. The only path to healing. The only way to understand what God had been trying to show me all along. And something unexpected happened: I didn't fall apart as I feared—I fell into grace.

That's what surrender does. It silences the lies you've believed. It shuts down the voice that says you're too broken. It replaces the labels the world gave you with the identity God already wrote. Once that happens—once you've tasted what it's like to let go of the steering wheel and trust God's hands instead of your own, the Bible starts reading you more than you read it. I used to show up with a highlighter and a checklist. Now I show up like someone looking for their next breath. That's why I keep coming back to Luke 9:23: *"Whoever wants to be my disciple must deny themselves and take up their cross daily and follow me."*

Maybe you've noticed that verse showing up throughout this book. That's no accident. Jesus said this more than once because He wasn't offering a motivational phrase—He was diagnosing our problem. You want to follow Me? Then you're going to have to die to yourself daily.

No wonder we resist it. But the life He offers—real life, full life, transformed life—only comes after surrender. Reading the Bible without surrender is like staring at a locked door and refusing to turn the key. You can appreciate it, admire it, talk about it, but you'll never walk through it until you let go. Surrender isn't what keeps you from the Bible—it's what unlocks it.

And it's not about reading more verses. It's about believing them. I'm not a scholar. I didn't go to seminary. I could barely quote Romans with a head start and an open Bible. But I got tired of faking it and finally let God in. And when I did, the words started making sense—not in my head, but in my soul. Stories that I thought I knew cracked open with meaning. Verses that I used to skim felt like they were written just for me. Even the hard ones started to soften me, not offend me. Surrender is what makes the Bible readable, not just intellectually, but personally.

Let's go even deeper. You probably didn't wake up one day and think, "Let's surrender control of every detail of my life to an invisible God." You likely grew into control out of fear, pain, or performance. Maybe it helped you survive, succeed, or hide. You can build your whole life on control and not realize how heavy it is—until it breaks you. That's why surrender rarely feels like a decision. It feels like a collapse. And not because God wants to crush you, but because He wants to rescue you.

Psalm 34:18 puts it this way: "*The Lord is close to the brokenhearted and saves those who are crushed in spirit.*" Not tolerates. Not advises. Saves. Your breakdown might be the beginning of your breakthrough. Surrender is saying, "God, I'm done playing God." It's not weakness—it's wisdom. And when you surrender, the Bible becomes the place where your real story begins. You start seeing yourself in people you once skipped past.

You're not just reading about the woman caught in adultery—you're feeling her shame and hearing Jesus say, "*Neither do I condemn you.*" You're not just analyzing Peter's denial; you're remembering your own. You're not just memorizing verses; you're meeting the Author.

Let's talk about shame. Because it's always nearby. Shame whispers: "You're too far gone. Too late. Too dumb. You should've known this stuff already." But surrender and shame can't coexist. One has to go. Surrender says, "I'm not enough, but God is." Shame says, "You're not enough, and you never will be."

If we don't learn to pause shame, we'll never press play on growth. Isaiah 54:4 says, "*Do not be afraid; you will not be put to shame.*" God said that to people who had rebelled, and He was still inviting them to come close. Romans 10:11 adds, "*Anyone who believes in him will never be put to shame.*" Shame is not your sentence; it's a lie.

The more you believe God wants you close—not cleaned up, just close—the easier surrender becomes. And the more you surrender, the more Scripture speaks. So, let's stop making excuses.

- Too busy? We scroll endlessly.
- Too tired? God wants willing hearts, not perfect ones.
- Too confused? We binge on entire TV series with tangled plotlines.

Deuteronomy 30:14 says, "*The word is very near you; it is in your mouth and in your heart so you may obey it.*" You don't read the Bible because you have it all together. You read it because you don't. We avoid the Bible not because of time or confusion, but because of fear. Fear that it will call us out. And it will—but only to call us home.

We don't want more guilt. We want transformation. Peace. Healing. Truth. All of it lives in God's Word—but only for the heart that's surrendered. Even when we know surrender is good, we still resist it. Why? Because surrender means giving up the story we've written about ourselves. And if that story has been shaped by shame, surrender can feel like giving up. But it's not giving up; it's giving over.

Isaiah 30:15 says, "*In repentance and rest is your salvation, in quietness and trust is your strength, but you would have none of it.*" Let that sink in. God offers rest, strength, and salvation, and they refused it. Why? Because surrender felt too still. Too passive. Too risky. They chose striving over surrender.

And we do, too. We don't like quiet. We like noise because it drowns out doubt. We don't like trust. We like results because we can measure those. But God doesn't meet us in hustle. He meets us in humility. 1 Peter 5:6 says, "*Humble yourselves, therefore, under God's mighty hand, that he may lift you up in due time.*" You want to rise? Go low. You want a breakthrough? Let go.

So, how do we surrender, practically? It's not about intensity; it's about intention. Not how loud you worship, but whether your Monday belongs to Him. Ask yourself:

- Am I reading to finish a chapter or to hear God?
- Am I praying to check in or to depend?
- Am I only letting God into the rooms I've cleaned up?

Surrender says, "Here are the keys. Every room. Even the one labeled **Do Not Enter**."

One final verse: "*Lord, I know that people's lives are not their own; it is not for them to direct their steps*" (Jeremiah 10:23). This one doesn't make many T-shirts, but maybe it should. That's surrender. The world says you're the captain. The Bible says you're not even supposed to drive. When you try, you may look like you're winning—until the crash.

I didn't surrender during quiet time with soft music. It came through collapse. Through grace. Now, we stand at the crossroads. Surrender isn't a new idea; it's stitched into Scripture. Abraham on the mountain. Jesus in Gethsemane. These aren't just Bible stories; they're mirrors. They show us what it looks like to trust when everything in us wants to run. And if surrender led them to peace . . . it will lead us there too.

# Chapter 17:
# WHEN TRUST COSTS EVERYTHING

## Abraham's Trust – The Story

*Absolute surrender is trusting God enough to place everything in His hands—even when we don't know how it will end.*

Abraham had waited a lifetime for Isaac to be born. Every day he watched the boy laugh and play, every meal a reminder of God's promise fulfilled. Isaac was not just a son; he was the living, breathing proof of a covenant God made long ago: "*I will make your descendants as numerous as the stars*" (Genesis 26:4). How many nights had Abraham stared into the vast sky, clinging to that promise?

So, when God's voice broke the quiet: "*Abraham!*" He answered instantly, "*Here I am.*" But the words that followed must have felt like a blade to his heart: "*Take your son, your only son, whom you love—Isaac—and go to the region of Moriah. Sacrifice him there as a burnt offering on a mountain I will show you*" (Genesis 22:2).

That night, Abraham surely lay awake, eyes open to the dark ceiling of his tent, every breath shallow. He must have watched Isaac sleep, remembering each milestone: Isaac's first cry, his tiny hand gripping his father's finger, his laughter as he learned to walk. How could God ask this? Why would God give a promise only to ask for its life? Was this the end of everything Abraham had waited for?

But as dawn broke, Abraham rose. His legs felt like stone as he split the wood for the offering, the axe falling in rhythm with the pounding of his heart. He saddled the donkey, gathered two servants, and gently woke Isaac—this beloved child who trusted him completely. Isaac rubbed the sleep from his eyes and smiled, completely unaware they were starting the longest journey of his father's life.

For three days, they walked. Three days in the silent wilderness, every sunrise a reminder that God had not changed His command. Every night around the campfire, Abraham must have stolen glances at Isaac across the flames, memorizing his face, listening to him breathe. Did Isaac chatter about the journey? Did he ask questions Abraham couldn't answer? Each moment must have felt like a cruel eternity; a countdown Abraham couldn't stop.

On the third day, the mountain appeared on the horizon. Abraham's heart must have thundered in his chest. He turned to his servants and said words thick with faith and agony: "*Stay here. . . . We will worship and then we will come back to you*" (Genesis 22:5). Did he believe it literally? Or did hope burn so fiercely he couldn't bear to speak of any other outcome?

He placed the wood on Isaac's back. They climbed together, step by painful step. Isaac's small voice broke the silence: "*Father?*" Abraham must have swallowed hard, fighting tears. "*Yes, my son?*" Isaac looked around and said, "*The fire and wood are here, . . . but where is the lamb for the burnt offering*" (Genesis 22:7)? Abraham's soul must have screamed inside him, but with quiet, trembling faith he whispered, "*God himself will provide the lamb, my son*" (Genesis 22:8).

Each footstep up the mountain felt heavier than the last. When they reached the place God had shown him, Abraham's hands must have been shaking as he built the altar. Each stone he stacked was a silent cry: God, please . . .

Then came the hardest moment of any father's life: Abraham tied his son's hands. Isaac, old enough to resist, did not. Did he understand? Did his eyes search his father's for answers? Did he see tears streaming down Abraham's cheeks as he laid him on the wood? Abraham reached for the knife. His breath must have come in ragged gasps as his heart pleaded with every beat: Lord, stop me. Please. But he raised his hand, ready to obey.

Then, at the very edge of the unthinkable, heaven broke in. "*Abraham! Abraham!*" He gasped, "*Here I am,*" his voice cracking with hope and relief. "*Do not lay a hand on the boy. . . . Now I know that you fear God, because you have not withheld from me your son, your only son*" (Genesis 22:12).

Abraham's knees must have given way as he looked up—and there, tangled in the thicket, stood a ram. Tears streamed down his face as he untied Isaac, hugging him with an intensity only a father can know. He sacrificed the ram instead, overwhelmed by awe and gratitude. He named the place *Jehovah Jireh*—The Lord Will Provide—because there on that mountain, God showed His faithfulness was stronger than any test.

God reaffirmed His covenant, swearing by Himself that Abraham's descendants would be as countless as the stars and sand, and that through his offspring, all nations would be blessed—because Abraham obeyed with total surrender.

## What Can We Learn from This Story of Abraham and Isaac?

Abraham's story shows us that real faith isn't measured by how eagerly we trust God for blessings, but by how deeply we trust Him when obedience costs us everything. God's intention wasn't to harm

Abraham but to reveal the beauty of surrender—a faith so radical it would echo through generations and prepare the world for the day God Himself would provide the Lamb.

This story teaches us that when we're willing to lay down what we hold most dear—our dreams, our security, even our most precious relationships—we create space for God to work in ways beyond what we could ever imagine. Abraham's willingness to place Isaac on the altar didn't lead to loss; it opened the door to God's breathtaking provision and the fulfillment of His promises.

This story still relevant today because we will face moments when God asks us to trust Him beyond what makes sense—to walk up our own mountains of surrender without knowing how it will end. Abraham's faith lights the path, reminding us that God's character can be trusted even when His plan is hidden.

Ultimately, Abraham's story points us to the bigger story: His willingness to offer Isaac foreshadows the gospel. Thousands of years later, God would provide His own Son—not just for one family, but for the entire world. Jesus, the true Lamb, would carry wood on His back and climb another hill, offering Himself as the final sacrifice to redeem us all. Abraham's test reveals God's heart: He is faithful, He provides, and His love is greater than any sacrifice He asks us to make.

In the end, Abraham's story calls us to hold every dream, every hope, and every gift with open hands before a God who keeps His promises. Because in surrender, we don't lose; we make room for a faith that changes not only our story, but the world around us.

## Jesus in the Garden – The Story

*Faith is not proven by what we receive, but by what we're willing to give back to the God who gave it.*

After the Passover meal, Jesus led His disciples through Jerusalem's darkened streets. The night air was thick with foreboding. They crossed the Kidron Valley, moonlight shimmering off its shallow waters, and stepped into Gethsemane—a quiet olive grove where Jesus had often prayed. But this night was different: The hour of His greatest trial had come.

He told His disciples, "*Sit here while I go over there and pray*" (Matthew 26:36). But He couldn't face this alone. He took Peter, James, and John deeper into the grove. His face was pale, His steps unsteady. "*My soul is overwhelmed with sorrow to the point of death. Stay here and keep watch with me*" (Matthew 26:38).

This wasn't the fearless Jesus who calmed storms and cast out demons. This was the fully human Son of God, feeling the suffocating terror of what awaited Him. He staggered a few steps away, then collapsed to the ground, His sweat dampening the earth beneath Him.

He poured out His heart to the Father: "*Father, if you are willing, take this cup from me; yet not my will, but yours be done*" (Luke 22:42). He trembled, not because of Roman whips or nails, but because He faced something far worse: the full weight of humanity's sin and separation from the Father He had known for eternity.

As He prayed, an angel appeared to strengthen Him (Luke 22:43), yet the agony only deepened. Luke records that His sweat became like drops of blood falling to the ground—a sign of unimaginable psychological and spiritual torment. The Son of God was literally hemorrhaging His anguish into the soil of Gethsemane.

He rose to check on His friends, longing for even a shred of comfort from the men who had pledged to follow Him to death. But each time, He found them asleep, exhausted from sorrow and oblivious to the cosmic battle raging a few steps away. "*Could you not keep watch with me for one hour?*" He asked Peter (Matthew 26:40).

His voice must have been tinged with heartbreak, not anger, with the pain of facing His loneliest hour alone.

Three times He returned to pour out His soul: *"Abba, Father . . . everything is possible for you. Take this cup from me. Yet not what I will, but what you will"* (Mark 14:36). Each time, He fought His dread with faith, surrendering more completely to the plan He knew was the only way to save us.

With each prayer, His resolve hardened—not in cold resignation, but in fierce, unstoppable love. By the third time He stood, something had shifted: The trembling was gone. His face set with holy determination, He woke His disciples. *"Are you still sleeping and resting? Enough! The hour has come. Look, the Son of Man is delivered into the hands of sinners. Rise! Let us go! Here comes my betrayer"* (Mark 14:41–42)!

In the flickering torchlight, Judas approached, leading soldiers and officials. Jesus stepped forward willingly—not as a victim dragged to His fate, but as the King who chose the cross, who had already won the fiercest battle in Gethsemane. The courage of the Son of God shone brighter than the full moon overhead.

## What Can We Learn from Jesus in the Garden?

Jesus in Gethsemane shows us that courage isn't the absence of fear; it's choosing obedience while trembling. His anguish reveals that faith doesn't ignore pain; it presses into it, stays present, and surrenders fully. In that garden, we see a Savior who knows our deepest dread, yet still says, *"Not my will, but Yours be done."* His surrender wasn't weakness; it was strength born in honest prayer and perfect trust.

God's intention was to reveal Jesus's full humanity alongside His divine purpose. Gethsemane reminds us that we don't need to pretend we're strong. We can bring our raw, broken prayers to God—our "take this cup" moments—and find grace waiting there.

Jesus didn't just teach surrender; He lived it. And in doing so, He became the Savior who understands, who suffers with us, and who finishes what we never could.

This story is still profoundly relevant because we all face nights like that—when the weight of what's ahead feels unbearable. Jesus shows us how to wrestle honestly, pray deeply, trust completely, and walk forward—step by surrendered step.

And this story tells us something life-changing: We are worth every drop of Jesus's agony, every tear, every moment of His surrender. His choice to drink the cup was the battle before the cross, where love shattered sin's grip and opened the way home. Gethsemane proves that God's love isn't passive or polite; it's fierce, sacrificial, and willing to suffer so we could live.

# Chapter 18:

# DESPERATION

*When a boy grows up believing he's unworthy, he becomes a man desperate to prove he matters—chasing approval like it's air, never realizing he's already suffocating.*

I had just finished what I believed God had written through me. I set down the final words, surprised by how the story had unfolded—amazed, really, that it was finished at all. But as I began to reread the manuscript, it became clear: I might have been finished, but He wasn't. God was still at work, and there were pieces of my story—of His story I hadn't told yet.

That realization hit me as I tried to convince myself the book was done. I kept feeling a nudge, like God was whispering that there were things I'd skipped over, parts I'd left out because they were hard or painful to share. And, like I've done more times than I'd like to admit, I ignored that nudge and decided to walk away.

That's when it happened. I was standing in our closet—of all places—when I just started singing: "Desperation is a long, long road." The words came out of nowhere and wouldn't leave me alone.

I went downstairs, grabbed my guitar, and more words poured out. Through missed chords and clumsy strumming, a melody took shape. Before I knew it, I had a complete song in my hands. I couldn't believe it.

The next couple of days were filled with restless edits as I tried to force the manuscript into feeling finished. But every change felt off, like I was trying to wrap up something that wasn't ready to end. By last night, I went to bed frustrated and defeated.

Then, early this morning, I woke up with those lyrics playing in my head like a record stuck on repeat. As I began to pray, it was as if God turned on a light inside me. He showed me, through the chapters I'd already written, that everything I'd been praying for over the years was unfolding right in front of me. I could see how He had been answering those prayers all along—I'd just been too busy writing my story to notice the one He was writing.

Just last night, I was so focused on crafting the words that I wasn't reading the story He was telling through my life. And maybe, as the reader, you could already see what was happening—how God was moving behind the scenes—while I completely missed it. That's because this book is alive. We're not just retelling old memories; we're witnessing Him work in real time, right here, right now.

This book isn't just about sharing my story—it's about sharing His. And it wasn't finished, because He wasn't finished. The prayers I'd whispered for years were starting to take shape before my eyes. The changes I'd longed for weren't just stories from the past—they were happening in the present. And to share that truth, I knew I'd have to be honest about the parts of my life I'd tried so hard to keep hidden.

So, no—the book wasn't finished. There was more of my story to tell, and more of God's story to reveal. And as the reader, you'll never see those rushed, empty chapters I tried to force; instead, you'll see what God intended all along: the truth He's been writing from the very beginning. As you're reading these words, you're witnessing that story as it's still being written. What started as a melody became a message—a song that I didn't realize was telling my story until much later. The song God gave me included these lyrics:

Desperation is a long, long road
Where the nights are cold, and the hope feels old
Every step echoes the fears I've sown
But I keep walking, I can't go home

I've called out into empty skies
Whispered prayers, nobody replies
But there's a spark I can't let die
A restless heart that's asking why

Oh, lead me where the light breaks through
Past the shadows I've clung to
Desperation won't define my soul
He'll find a way to make me whole

I've been walking a road of desperation for most of my life—a road paved with the need to prove myself, to silence the voices that said I'd never measure up, to rewrite the story I thought defined me.

When God gave me these lyrics, I did what I've done so many times before: I scribbled them down, put them to music, and thought, *Well, that's a nice song—what's next?* I didn't pause to ask what He was trying to show me.

But this morning, God opened my eyes. He showed me that these lyrics weren't just words; they were a mirror reflecting my life. Like this book, where my story weaves with His, these lyrics were His way of revealing the truth I'd missed: I've spent years on a road of desperation because I let everyone else define me, except the One who created me.

The nights were cold. Hope did feel old. I realized it was because I wasn't renewing my hope in His Word. Isaiah 40:31 says, "*But those who hope in the Lord will renew their strength.*" But I'd been hoping in myself, in my performance, in proving I was enough, and I was exhausted because those things can't renew anything.

Every fear I carried was planted by lies—stories others told me about who I was or wasn't. Jesus says in John 8:32, "*Then you will know the truth, and the truth will set you free.*" But I was living in everyone else's version of the truth, and it kept me chained up, marching down a road that felt like it would never end.

I kept walking—no way home, or so I thought. But God was there the whole time. He showed me this morning that the skies weren't empty, that my whispered prayers didn't bounce off the ceiling. He heard every word. That spark that wouldn't die, the restless heart that kept asking why—that was Him. He planted it. He kept it alive, even when I was convinced, I'd lost all hope.

And when the time was right, He led me where the light broke through. He took me past the shadows I'd been clinging to—the old lies, the old fears, the old shame. He showed me that desperation doesn't define my soul because He already does. He found a way to make me whole, just like He promised in Psalm 34:18: "*The Lord is close to the brokenhearted and saves those who are crushed in spirit.*"

Here's the truth: God used every twist and turn in my story, every failure, every wrong turn, and every desperate step to bring me to this very moment. He knew exactly where I'd run, how far I'd go, and when I'd finally stop. And when I got there, He wasn't just waiting—He'd been watching me with love and patience I can't begin to understand.

Now I know I can't finish this book without telling the part of my story I wanted to hide. Because if I don't share it, I'm not just holding back my story—I'm holding back His. This book didn't start with a plan or have a set ending—just a desire to show how reading God's Word changes everything. I began by telling my story. But sharing the whole truth isn't easy, especially knowing people I love might read it. Some stories have a dark side, and this is mine.

Depression is something I've battled my entire life. There have been very few things that have brought me real, lasting joy—and honestly, those joys are probably the most obvious ones: my wife, my daughters, my grandchildren, and a few good friends who know exactly who they are. Without these people, I can't imagine what my life would look like; they've been my lifelines in some of my darkest moments.

Talking about depression is hard, and I don't pretend to be an expert. If I am an expert in anything, it's only in my own experience—because I've lived it, felt it, and wrestled with it more times than I can count. But for the sake of understanding, let's take a quick look at what the experts say about depression:

- Depression is more than sadness. It's a serious mental health condition that affects how you feel, think, and handle daily activities. It's like a fog that settles over your life, making even simple things feel impossible.
- Symptoms can include feeling hopeless or worthless, losing interest in things you once enjoyed, changes in sleep or appetite, constant fatigue, difficulty concentrating, and sometimes thoughts of self-harm.
- Depression can have many causes. It can stem from brain chemistry, genetics, trauma, chronic stress, or difficult life circumstances. It's not a sign of weakness, and you can't just "snap out of it."
- Treatment helps. Therapy, medication, lifestyle changes, and support from loved ones can make a huge difference. You don't have to fight alone.

In simple terms, depression is like carrying an invisible weight that you can't set down. It makes every step feel harder, every day feel longer, and every hope feel more distant. But you're not alone, and you're not beyond help.

In even simpler terms: depression sucks.

I've spent more nights than I can count lying awake, wondering why God gave me breath in the first place. I mean, He had the perfect opportunity to call it quits before it even started—I didn't breathe for four minutes when I was born. Four minutes! Why give me that first gasp at all if this was what living was going to feel like?

As a kid, I remember this heavy sadness hanging over me like a storm cloud that never moved on, especially when I was alone. It was in those quiet moments, when the world went still, that the voice in my head would start whispering: What's the point? You're never going to amount to anything anyway.

And here's the thing—it wasn't just the words people spoke over me. Sure, hearing "you're worthless" hurts, but it went deeper. Even if no one had said it, I think I would've felt worthless anyway. It was like worthlessness had taken up permanent residence in my chest.

I tried to avoid being alone at all costs. And for a while, it worked. Being around people was like a temporary anesthetic—I felt lighter, less haunted. I discovered early on that if I could make people laugh, even just a chuckle, I felt a little better. It was like I'd stumbled on a secret superpower: If I could get someone else to forget their pain for a minute, maybe I could forget mine too.

Besides, I've always loved seeing people laugh. There's just something about laughter that's contagious and healing—even if, deep down, I was the one who needed healing most. The pain didn't get easier as I got older—in fact, it got harder to hide. I started to wonder if maybe this was just who I was meant to be: someone broken. But then I thought, *What if I could rewrite the story?* And

I had plenty of reasons for wanting to rewrite it—this was just one more. If I could become someone else entirely, maybe the pain would finally let me go. So, I tried to write my own story—because if I had to be someone, at least I could choose who that person would be.

School was probably the hardest chapter of that story. When you're bad at something—anything—you look for ways to compensate. My way was laughter. If I could make people laugh, even just for a moment, I felt like I was winning. Because when you're truly laughing, nothing else matters. Think about it—when you're doubled over giggling, are you worried about the bills that are due, the job you hate, or the person who cut you off in traffic? Of course not. In that moment, you're free.

I craved that freedom. I needed it. But the distraction of chasing laughter came at a cost: incomplete schoolwork, homework assignments that never got turned in, and grades that slipped through my fingers. There were a lot of reasons for that—some I understood then; others I've only begun to realize now. But to my teachers, it just looked like I had too much energy or couldn't sit still. They didn't see the pain I was trying desperately to escape. Because when you stop moving, stop joking, stop distracting yourself, the pain rushes back instantly, and I couldn't bear to sit in that darkness. I just wanted it to go away.

Sometimes, people can't see the real problem. Other times, they don't want to see it—or worse, they just don't care. And so, I kept performing, kept laughing, kept distracting, trying to survive in a world that didn't understand how much it hurt just to be me.

You can't explain the pain of depression in a way that lets someone who's never felt it truly understand. And *pain* isn't even the right word. Pain sounds physical, like a cut or a bruise. Depression is more like anguish—a suffocating weight pressing down on your chest, a constant ache in your soul, a feeling that you'd do anything, absolutely anything, just to make it stop.

When I was younger, I didn't think much about suicide. Honestly, I was too busy trying to outrun my feelings to even name them. But before I go any further, we need to talk about it—because if you're reading this and you or someone you know is thinking about ending their life, I beg you: Put this book down right now and reach out to someone. There is help. I know it might feel hopeless in this moment, but I promise there are people who care and will do everything they can to help you. If you don't know where to start, call or text **988**—the Suicide and Crisis Lifeline. They're available 24/7.

Okay—deep breath—let's keep going.

I spent years looking for ways to feel better. I thought if I could prove everyone wrong or show the people who believed the worst about me that I was smart enough, strong enough, good enough, then maybe I'd finally feel okay. Spoiler alert: That plan didn't work. Instead, I spent most of my time confused, lost, and too embarrassed to talk to anyone about how I felt. How do you start that conversation? "Hi, I'm drowning on dry land . . . how's your day going?"

So why am I telling you this now? Why spill my guts in the middle of a book about the Bible? Two big reasons:

1.  The Bible—the very reason for this book—talks about everything we're going through. If, after accepting Christ, I'd dug into His Word, I could have learned things that would have changed everything sooner. The Bible says:
    *   "*The* LORD *is close to the brokenhearted and saves those who are crushed in spirit*" (Psalm 34:18). He sees you.
    *   "*Cast all your anxiety on him because he cares for you*" (1 Peter 5:7). He wants you to unload your fears on Him.

- *"Come to me, all you who are weary and burdened, and I will give you rest"* (Matthew 11:28). He offers rest no one else can give.

The Bible reminds us we're not alone, that our feelings don't make us faithless, and that God can handle our hardest days.

2. If you're battling depression right now, I want you to know that you don't have to fight alone. There are people who want to help—people who've been where you are and made it through. Please don't keep it to yourself. Talk to someone. Share with a friend, a counselor, your pastor, or your doctor. If you're a parent, ask your kids what they're feeling—really ask. Don't assume you know what's going on inside them. And please, don't rush to medicate before you understand the root of what they're struggling with. Depression is complex, and everyone's story is different.

Here's the truth: Depression lies. It says you're alone, but you're not. It says things will never get better, but they can. And it says you don't matter, but you do—more than you know.

Remember, if you or someone you love needs help right now, you can call or text **988** in the US to reach the Suicide and Crisis Lifeline 24/7.

Depression was something I never talked to my wife about—not until much later in our marriage, when things had gotten so bad I couldn't keep it hidden anymore. It's strange, because on paper, I had the kind of life most men would envy. (And yes, I know envy is a sin—so let's just call that what it is. But if you can't laugh a little while unpacking decades of emotional baggage, you're probably going to cry the whole time.)

Seriously, though, my life looked great from the outside. I had a wife who loved me and treated me better than I ever deserved. And I don't say that lightly. I could go on and on about what an incredible woman she is, but you'd probably accuse me of bragging. Then there were our two beautiful, smart, mostly well-behaved daughters—let's be honest, no one's perfect, but they were as close as it gets. And I had a solid job, the kind people spend their whole careers hoping to find.

So why couldn't I find joy? It seems like a simple question, but it wasn't. It was deeper than I was ready—or willing—to explore back then. The truth was, I was hurting in a way I couldn't explain. And I definitely couldn't tell my wife what I was feeling, because how do you say, "I know you love me and everything looks great, but inside I feel like I'm falling apart," without sounding weak, broken, or worthless? That's how I saw it, anyway.

She would ask me, gently but persistently: "Is there something I'm not doing? Something you need that I'm not giving you? Why aren't you happy?" And every time she asked, it broke my heart. It cut through me like a blade of guilt—sharp, deep, and impossible to ignore. Because in those moments, I saw what she couldn't: She thought it was her. She believed she wasn't enough. And that shattered me, because the truth was, she was perfect—she was my everything. She and the girls were the only reasons I hadn't done something I couldn't take back.

I was the problem. But my silence made her believe she was the problem. And what about our girls? Did they think Dad wasn't happy because of them? Did they wonder if they weren't enough, either? That thought was unbearable. I couldn't keep putting my brokenness onto the people I loved most. They didn't deserve to carry the weight of my pain.

I knew something had to change because the silence was hurting them as much as it was destroying me.

One day, I did the unthinkable. I came home from work and backed into our garage. I knew my wife wouldn't be home for hours. I closed the garage door behind me, turned off my phone, and just sat there with the engine running. I was done. Done hurting the people I loved. Done carrying an anguish I couldn't even describe. It felt like the only way to end the pain, for me and everyone else.

I sat there for what felt like forever as the exhaust fumes grew thicker, the smell filling the car, the air heavy and sour. And as awful as it sounds, there was a sense of grim relief washing over me—like the feeling you get when you've listened to a leaky faucet drip . . . drip . . . drip . . . for years, and then you finally tighten it just right and the dripping stops. That suffocating silence felt like peace, like I'd finally quieted the relentless noise in my head.

The silence I thought would bring peace was actually the darkness lying to me . . .

And then, just like that, I reached over and turned off the car. I wasn't going to do that to my family. That wasn't the legacy I wanted to leave behind. But if I'm completely honest, it shook me to my core. Because what if it hadn't been exhaust fumes? What if I'd chosen something faster—something that wouldn't have given me a chance to second-guess myself? I know in my heart that if I'd had a more immediate means, there might not have been time to change my mind, and everything would be different today. That's God's grace—plain and simple.

Afterward, I told my wife everything. I needed her to know it was never about her. She and the girls were my reason for living— they were the reason I reached over and turned that car off. I could never bring myself to share all of it with my daughters; some truths are just too heavy. But talking to my wife was a lifeline. She knew. She started holding me accountable, checking on me, making sure I wasn't fighting this battle alone.

I also sought professional help. I saw a psychologist, and for a while, I took medication. It turned out the meds weren't effective for me, but the conversations—opening up about my pain—and giving it to the Lord were what truly helped me begin to heal.

Depression is personal. It doesn't look the same for everyone, and it can't be treated the same way for everyone either. That's why seeking help is always the first step—talking to someone who knows how to walk you through it, whether that's a counselor, a doctor, or someone you trust. Because no one should have to carry this burden alone.

The song the Lord gave me finishes like this:

> I've been down on broken knees
> Dreaming of a dawn I've yet to see
>
> But faith is born when night is black
> And love can call the lost one back
> So, lead me where the light breaks through
> Past the ghosts that I once knew
>
> Desperation won't define my soul
> I'm stronger now, I'm letting go

I've been down on broken knees, my heart pounding and my mind screaming as I asked God why He let me live when I was so ready to give up. I've dreamed of a better day, longing desperately to see a dawn that felt like it would never come. In the pitch-black night of my soul—when I truly believed taking my life was the only escape—God's love reached deeper than my despair and called this lost, shattered heart back home.

He didn't just save me; He led me to where the light finally breaks through the suffocating darkness. He walked me past the ghosts of my past—the fear that paralyzed me, the pain that kept me captive, the shame that told me I'd never be enough. Those desperate moments, as real and raw as they were, don't get the final word over my life. God does.

I'm stronger now—not because the path was easy, but because of what God brought me through. Desperation won't define my soul anymore. I am letting go of the weight I carried for so long, and I'm learning to walk freely in the light of His love, knowing every breath I have is a gift of grace.

I didn't see it yesterday, but by God's grace, I see it today: This song tells my story—the story of chains broken, pain redeemed, and shame and guilt that Jesus now carries for me. It's about the peace and joy only He can give, and the healing found in His Word. God's Word shows us who He truly is.

So now, let's turn our ears to God's story. We've seen how desperation can bring us to our knees, but it can also open our hearts to the only One who can truly heal and restore. As we step into the next chapter, we'll meet others who found themselves desperate beyond hope, like the woman who bled for twelve years and the barren Hannah who wept bitterly for a child.

Their stories aren't just ancient tales; they're living proof that God meets us in our desperation with compassion and power. They show us that crying out isn't weakness—it's the beginning of a breakthrough. That surrender isn't failure—it's the foundation of freedom. And that the road of desperation, though long and often dark, is not a dead end. It's a path that leads straight to the heart of God.

Let's lean in and discover what their stories reveal about the God who sees us, hears us, and answers cries born from the deepest places of our hearts.

# Chapter 19:

# WHEN DESPERATION TOUCHES GOD

*Desperation led her to Jesus when nothing else could, and faith made her reach for the miracle only He could give.*

## The Desperate Woman – Story

She had been bleeding for twelve years. Every morning, she woke to the same dread: the ache in her body, the stain on her clothes, the crushing loneliness. She remembered what it felt like to be hugged, to join her friends at the well, to stand beside others in worship—those days felt like a lifetime ago. Now, she was a ghost on the edges of life, unclean, untouchable, and invisible.

Doctors promised hope but only took her last coins. Each failed treatment drained more than her savings; it drained her spirit. She began to believe what people whispered behind her back—that she was cursed, abandoned, forgotten even by God.

Then came stories of Jesus. A healer who touched lepers. A teacher who welcomed sinners. A man who claimed to carry God's power and compassion. Could it be true? Could He love someone like her?

When Jesus came to town, the streets overflowed with people desperate for a glimpse. She wrapped her shawl tightly around her face, her heart hammering. Shame screamed, *Stay hidden*! But hope whispered, *Reach for Him*.

From the accounts detailed in the Gospels of Luke and Mark, we can paraphrase a narrative of this desperate woman's story. She forced her way through the crush of bodies, her breath ragged, the world narrowing to one thought: If I can just touch His robe . . .

Her hand darted out. In that single heartbeat, her fingers grazed the edge of His cloak—and instantly, warmth spread through her body. The bleeding stopped. Strength filled her limbs. Tears welled up—she hadn't felt this alive in years.

Then He stopped. He turned in the crowd, eyes searching. "Who touched Me?" His voice was gentle, but it pierced her soul. Panic surged. She tried to shrink away, but hiding was impossible now.

The disciples scoffed. "Lord, everyone's pressing in on You." But Jesus insisted, "Someone touched Me; I know that power has gone out from Me." She fell at His feet, trembling, sobbing without sound, confessing the whole truth—her years of suffering, her hopelessness, the risk she took, the instant miracle.

Silence fell over the crowd as Jesus looked at her—not with anger, but with eyes full of tender love. He spoke words she never imagined hearing: *"Daughter, your faith has healed you. Go in peace and be freed from your suffering"* (Mark 5:34).

In a moment, she was more than healed; she was seen, valued, and restored. Jesus didn't just cure her body—He gave her back her dignity, identity, and a future filled with peace.

## What Can We Learn from the Bleeding Woman's Story?

The story of the bleeding woman reveals that true faith often grows in desperation, when we've exhausted every other option and realize that Jesus is our only hope. Her small, trembling act of reaching for His robe shows that even the faintest step of faith can move the heart of God and release His power. Jesus didn't just heal her body; He restored her identity by calling her "Daughter," reminding us that we are not defined by our pain, past, or shame, but by our relationship with Him.

This story is still powerfully relevant today. Many of us carry hidden wounds and silent shame that isolate us from others and from God. This woman's faith invites us to push past fear and reach for Jesus, trusting that He sees us and knows our suffering and that He will respond with compassion. Her story also points to the greater mission of Jesus—to restore the broken, redeem the rejected, and carry our shame to the cross so we can be made whole. Woven into God's greater story of salvation, the bleeding woman's encounter reminds us that faith in Jesus heals, restores, and invites us into the family of God.

Just as one woman reached through the crowd to touch Jesus, another fell to her knees years earlier, begging God for what only He could give.

## Hannah's Desperation – The Story

*Hannah's tears weren't a sign of weakness—they were the seeds of a miracle. She poured out her soul to God, and He filled her arms with the answer only He could give.*

Hannah's days were a constant ache of longing. Though married to Elkanah, who loved her dearly and tried to comfort her, she couldn't shake the emptiness in her heart—or in her arms. Month after month, year after year, she waited for the day she'd feel the stirrings of life within her womb, only to face disappointment again and again.

Adding to her torment was Peninnah, Elkanah's other wife, who had children and delighted in reminding Hannah of what she lacked. At every meal, every family gathering, Peninnah's words stung like poison: "God has blessed me—why hasn't He blessed you?" Her cruel taunts echoed in Hannah's mind, amplifying her feelings of shame and worthlessness.

Elkanah, though loving, didn't fully understand. He once asked her, "*Hannah, why are you weeping? Why don't you eat? Why are you downhearted? Don't I mean more to you than ten sons*" (1 Samuel 1:8)? His words were meant to comfort, but they reminded Hannah of the chasm between her pain and his understanding.

Every year, their family traveled to Shiloh to worship and sacrifice to the Lord. The journey should have been one of hope, but for Hannah, it was another reminder of her barrenness. Yet she kept going—faithfully bringing her broken heart to the house of God.

One year, unable to contain her grief, she slipped away to the temple and fell on her knees. Her body shook with silent sobs as she prayed so intensely her lips moved without sound. Her heart's cry poured out like water before God: "*Lord Almighty, if you will only look on your servant's misery and remember me, and not forget your servant but give her a son, then I will give him to the Lord for all the days of his life*" (1Samuel 1:11).

The priest Eli saw her praying so passionately without speaking and thought she was drunk. He rebuked her, but Hannah, desperate and humiliated, explained: "I am a woman who is deeply troubled. . . . I was pouring out my soul to the Lord" (1 Samuel 1:15). Her words must have surprised Eli, for he softened and blessed her: "*Go in peace, and may the God of Israel grant you what you have asked of him*" (1 Samuel 1:17).

A quiet peace settled over Hannah's heart. She rose from the temple, wiped her tears, and went back to her family. For the first time in a long time, she ate and felt hope stirring where only emptiness had lived.

In time, God remembered Hannah's plea. He blessed her with a son, Samuel, whose name means "heard by God." True to her vow, once Samuel was weaned, she brought him back to Shiloh. With both gratitude and heartbreak, she handed him over to Eli to serve the Lord all his life.

Hannah's joy overflowed into a beautiful prayer of praise, a song of worship that declared God's greatness, His power to lift the humble, and His faithfulness to those who trust Him. Through Samuel, God would change the course of Israel's history, proving that Hannah's desperate prayer wasn't just heard—it was part of God's greater plan for His people.

## What Can We Learn from Hannah's Story?

Hannah's story reminds us that true faith is often born in seasons of sorrow, when we stop hiding our pain and pour our hearts out honestly before God. Her desperate, persistent prayers show that God welcomes our raw emotions and hears every unspoken cry. Even when misunderstood or dismissed by others, Hannah clung to hope, and God responded with compassion, not just answering her prayer but weaving her into His greater plan.

Her faith teaches us that our worth isn't found in what we have or lack, but in God's love and purpose for us. In a world where it's easy to feel forgotten, Hannah's story reminds us that we are fully seen, deeply valued, and never beyond His reach. Her trust, even when hope felt distant, encourages us to keep seeking God—because His timing is perfect, and our surrendered hearts can be used for something far greater than we imagine.

By giving her son Samuel back to the Lord, Hannah became part of God's plan to raise up a prophet who would shape the future of Israel and prepare the way for the coming Messiah. Her story points forward to Jesus—the ultimate answer to every desperate cry—showing that God hears, He remembers, and He works through ordinary people to accomplish extraordinary things.

# Chapter 20:
# WHEN GOD CORNERS YOU

*I asked God to change me. He said, "Okay—but hand over the wheel first." Turns out, surrender isn't just the path to transformation. It's the price.*

J ust five years from retirement, my life finally seemed . . . stable. Our girls were grown and raising families of their own. We were grandparents—three incredible grandsons and one beautiful little granddaughter who stole my heart and still hasn't given it back. We had moved a few times with my job, but now we had settled in Minnesota and planted in a solid church; we were surrounded by people we loved, and it felt like we were right where we were supposed to be.

On paper? Life looked good. Scratch that—life was good.

A loving marriage that had lasted over four decades (okay, mostly because my wife is amazing, but I helped). Two strong, smart, kind daughters (again . . . probably her influence, but let's not split hairs). A long career that provided for my family. Friends. Church. Laughter. Roots.

From the outside, I looked like the guy who made it. But on the inside? That scared little boy was still in there—hiding in a corner, holding his breath, terrified someone might finally see the truth: That I was stupid. That I was broken. That I wasn't enough.

I had gotten good at hiding him. Years of practice. I knew how to look like the guy who had it all together. I wore success like a shield and humor like a smoke bomb. If I could keep people smiling, they wouldn't look too closely. And most days, that worked. But some days . . . it didn't.

Some days, that old voice would sneak back in like a stray cat you fed once, and now it lives on your porch. "You're not really healed. . . . If they really knew you. . . . You're still that kid."

I had everything I thought I needed—church, prayer, men's groups, Bible studies. I had Jesus. But that voice still knew how to rob me. And I couldn't understand why. I prayed for transformation. I prayed for peace. I begged God to silence the lies once and for all. I'd close my eyes in prayer and open them, still carrying the same weight. Still haunted by the same fear: "What if they ever see the real me?"

Here's the thing: I looked at my Bible, but I didn't read it. I flipped through verses like spiritual fortune cookies. I highlighted Scriptures that sounded good. I listened to sermons. I read books about the Bible. But I didn't open the Word and say, "God, speak to me."

Because deep down . . . I was afraid of what He might say. I didn't want answers. I wanted comfort. But what I needed—what I had been avoiding—was truth.

I didn't need another devotional or another Bible study workbook. I needed the Bible itself. Not just as a source of inspiration, but as the scalpel God would use to finally cut through the lies, I'd believed for decades. That was the problem.

God hadn't failed to change me. I had failed to surrender to the way He wanted to change me. And that way always begins with His

Word. Here's the thing. I think Satan's fine with us skimming the Bible. I think he loves it. Because when we skim, we trick ourselves into thinking we're in God's Word . . . when we're not. We tell ourselves, "Well, I read a verse today, or "I heard a great sermon." But that's like reading the ingredients on a medicine bottle and expecting to be healed.

That kind of halfway-in approach doesn't draw us closer to the truth. It inoculates us against it. It gives us just enough exposure to think we're safe, but not enough to change us. Let me put it this way: Imagine a man who's sick and dying, but instead of taking the full treatment the doctor prescribed, he just rubs the pill bottle on his chest and says, "That should do it." He never swallows medicine. Never lets it get inside him. He just touches it—and wonders why he's still sick.

That's what skimming the Bible is like. We keep the truth close, but not close enough to let it in. We stroke the surface of Scripture but never open our hearts to it. Satan's not worried about you owning a Bible. He's worried about you opening it. He's worried about you reading it in full sentences, with full surrender, and letting it speak to the parts of you that no sermon can reach.

A little truth, halfway digested, can be more dangerous than none at all—because it convinces us we're fine when we're still bleeding. That's where I was. And honestly? That's where a lot of us are.

Somewhere along the way, we accepted Christ, but transformation? That never quite showed up. We believed in Jesus, maybe even got baptized, joined a small group . . . but we're still walking around carrying the same shame, the same lies, the same old pain we've had since childhood. And nobody talks about it. Because we've gotten really good at pretending.

We pray for transformation. We ask to be better—better husbands, wives, parents, people. But nothing seems to change. And when that happens, we do what we know how to do: We perform. We say the right things: "God is good. . . . Praise the Lord. . . .

I'll pray for you." But deep down? We're frustrated. We're tired of asking God to heal what still hurts. And when He doesn't fix it the way we expected, we start to wonder: Is this really working?

That question hits harder than we want to admit. "Do I really believe, or am I just hoping this is all real?" Because if it's not—if He's not—then what? What am I doing this for? Where's my hope supposed to go then? That's the quiet crisis of lukewarm Christianity. The part no one talks about. But Jesus did: *"So, because you are lukewarm—neither hot nor cold—I am about to spit you out of my mouth"* (Revelation 3:16).

That verse always hit me hard. I mean, come on—being ignored is bad. Being judged is worse. But being spit out? That's next-level. That's not just, "I'm disappointed in you." That's, "You make me gag."

And here's the scary part: Lukewarm doesn't look like it is broken. It looks . . . Christian. It shows up to church. It knows how to bow its head. It volunteers, sometimes. It says all the right things when people are watching. But deep down, it's bitter. It's worn down. It's tired of praying the same prayers and getting no answers. It starts to quietly resent God for not changing anything, and even worse, starts pretending nothing needs to change.

That was me. For years. I looked the part. I did the things. I had the life. But I still had this low-grade fear burning in the background: God's not really going to change me. He hasn't. Maybe He won't. And yet, I kept begging: Take the lies out of my head, God; make me new; help me believe I'm enough. But nothing happened. At least . . . not on the surface because here's the truth, I was missing:

- A little bit of God's Word won't change your life.
- A little bit of faith won't transform your identity.
- A little bit of surrender isn't surrender at all.
- Skimming the Bible and calling it devotion is like licking a vitamin and wondering why you're still sick.

It gives us just enough of the illusion of obedience to keep us from the real thing.

Satan's perfectly happy for you to flip a verse a day, say a quick prayer, and live your whole life one inch away from transformation—as long as you never actually give God everything. He's fine with us having "*a form of godliness but denying its power*" (2 Timothy 3:5). Because if you look spiritual but never actually surrender, you stay stuck—looking the part but missing the point.

Because surrender is where the change happens—not in performance, not in pretending, not in shallow prayers with no follow-through. It happens when we finally trust Him enough to let Him undo us—completely. It's all or nothing. That's the theme of this book. That's the theme of the gospel. And that's the decision every one of us has to make: Do I really trust God, or am I just hoping He exists?

Trust is the dividing line between performing faith and transforming faith. One keeps you busy; the other makes you new. The bottom line? I didn't trust God. Oh, I wanted His blessing. I wanted His help. I just didn't want Him driving.

But I knew something dangerous: The minute I opened God's Word—really opened it, one of two things was going to happen. Either I'd find no truth, and everything I'd believed would collapse—and I'd lose all hope. Or I'd find the truth, and it would wreck me—in the best way.

Because here's the thing: I've seen it happen. I've watched people change—really change—because of Scripture. People who used to be just as bitter, broken, and tangled in shame as I was were transformed. You know why? Because they did the work; they trusted God; they let the Word read them, not the other way around.

And the truth that so many of us avoid—the reason transformation feels out of reach—is this: You can't be transformed without surrender. And you can't surrender while still gripping the wheel. If God can't drive, He's not in the car; He's a hood ornament on your road trip to nowhere.

Sometimes, the Lord sees our desperation and answers. But not always the way we hoped. You know that saying, "Be careful what you pray for"? Yeah. That one. Turns out, God listens when you pray things like, "Lord, I just want to trust You more," or "Please change me," or my personal favorite, "Use me however You want." I imagine God hearing that and saying, "Okay, but don't freak out when I take the wheel—and the transmission—and all four tires."

Because here's the truth: He'll let you take the wheel just long enough to corner yourself. To run out of gas. To get stuck in the kind of spiritual cul-de-sac where your only options are crash . . . or call out to Him. And eventually—after four decades of white-knuckling my life, I gave up. I didn't raise the white flag in a church service or during an altar call. No, God cornered me somewhere between desperation and burnout. He stripped away every excuse I'd been using to avoid surrender—every reason, every delay, every "I'll get to it later." And He did it with a surgical level of love. Let me walk you through it.

As I said earlier, I was five years from retirement—five years from *the plan*. The one I'd carefully pieced together over an entire career. The one I believed would reward all my hard work with peace, comfort, and control. But then the company I worked for was acquired by a new firm, and it became painfully clear that five more years wasn't going to happen. The new leadership had different ideas, and I wasn't in them.

At first, I was frustrated. Angry, even. My plan was unraveling, and I felt like the rug had been pulled out from under me. But the truth? That plan was never really about retirement. It was about control. It was about hiding. I had spent years trying to prove something—maybe to others, maybe to myself. I'm still not sure who I was trying to impress. Most of the people I was striving to look good for weren't even paying attention. But God was.

And when my plan fell apart, His was just getting started. We moved to Missouri not long after that. We had an opportunity to be close to our youngest daughter and grandsons . . . then the next wave hit. After a lifetime of good health—never calling in sick, never missing work, rarely slowing down, I was diagnosed with something I had never heard of: *warm autoimmune hemolytic anemia*. It's a rare blood disorder in which the immune system goes rogue and starts destroying its own red blood cells. To say that this diagnosis wrecked me would be putting it lightly.

Breathing became a chore. Walking across the room felt like climbing a mountain. I had no energy. No stamina. My body was shutting down, and there wasn't a cure—just a cocktail of powerful medications and regular infusions to keep the symptoms in check. I felt helpless in a way I had never experienced before. And for someone who had always been the "push through it" guy, that helplessness hit hard.

Suddenly, I wasn't working. I wasn't striving. I wasn't performing. I wasn't "doing" anything. I was still. And that's when God moved. It was as if He said, "You're not going to sit down on your own? Okay. I'll help you with that." He didn't do it to punish me. He did it to free me. He removed every distraction, every excuse, every reason I'd been clinging to in order to avoid the one thing He'd been asking of me all along: full surrender.

No more, "I'll get to it later." No more hiding behind productivity or spiritual half-measures. There I was—with nothing but time, nothing but stillness, and nothing but my Bible . . . and breath. And honestly, I wasn't even sure how long I'd have either.

So I opened the Bible. And I didn't just read it casually. I devoured it. I studied it. I sat with it. And it *wrecked me*—in the best way. For the first time, I didn't just see rules or stories. I saw a rescue. I saw a love letter from a Father who'd been pursuing me all along. I found the answers I'd been searching for my whole life—not in a sermon, not in a plan, not in self-help—but in His Word.

God had allowed sickness to touch my body, so He could heal something far deeper in me. That's how much He loves us. Months passed. Slowly, my health improved. The disease isn't cured, but it's managed. Life started looking "normal" again. But God wasn't done.

Although I was finally reading His Word, He knew I still hadn't given Him everything. I was *close*. I was faithful. I was willing. But I still wasn't *surrendered*. And He loved me too much to stop halfway. He allowed it because He loves me enough not to let me stay stuck. And He loves you that much, too. What He did for me, He can do for you. But first, you've got to stop driving.

Look, the real story—the one that changed everything for me—is in the next chapter. It's the turning point. And we'll get there. But before we do, I need you to hear something that matters more than my story: God wrote this book. Yeah, I know my name is on the cover, but I'm just the pen. He's the Author. And if anything in these pages has been uncomfortable, convicting, or too close for comfort, take it up with Him.

Because the truth needs to be told. Stop blaming God when you don't see transformation in your life. Stop accusing Him of being silent when you haven't opened the one place He's been speaking from the whole time. I get it—maybe you're tired of hearing about surrender.

Maybe you think I've been a little too pushy. Maybe you're ready to chuck this book across the room and go back to scrolling social media. But here's the deal: Surrender isn't optional. It's the way out. The way forward. The way free.

Sometimes, God tries to get our attention gently. Other times, He corners us like a dad teaching his kid how to ride a bike: "You wanna steer? Okay . . . just know I'm letting go." We all know the old joke, but it's worth repeating:

> A man's drowning in the ocean and prays,
> "God, save me!"
> A cruise ship comes by and tosses him a rope.
> He waves it off: "No thanks, I'm waiting for God."
> Then a Coast Guard helicopter shows up—
> spotlight, harness, the whole deal.
> "Nope, still waiting on God."
> Finally, a yacht rolls past, big enough to throw a
> party on.
> Again, he refuses: "God's going to save me."
> He dies.
> When he gets to heaven, he asks God, "Why didn't
> You save me?"
> And God says, "I sent you two ships and a
> helicopter, genius."

Here's the point: Sometimes, the answer is right in front of you. Sometimes, the lifeline is already in your hands. And sometimes, God corners you not to punish you, but to rescue you. Brothers and sisters, the Bible is your lifeline. Stop waiting for a voice from heaven when He's already given you a book full of them:

> Open it.
> Read it.
> Let it read you.
> Let it wreck you.
> Let it rebuild you.

And if you can't seem to make yourself open the Bible . . . well, you're not the first. You'd be surprised how many people in Scripture had to be shoved, shaken, or shouted at by God just to pay attention. Take Pharaoh, for example. God sent frogs, flies, and full-on plagues, and the man still wouldn't budge. Or Balaam—God had to speak through a donkey just to get his attention. (You know it's bad when the donkey is the voice of reason.)

So, if you've ever been stubborn, slow to listen, or spiritually hard of hearing, you're in good company. Let's take a look.

# Chapter 21:
# CORNERED BY CONTROL

## Pharaoh – The Story

*When pride builds a throne in your heart, God will shake the ground beneath it—not to destroy you, but to free you from what was never meant to rule you.*

Pharaoh was the most powerful man in the known world. In Egypt, he wasn't just royalty—he was considered a god. Untouchable. Unquestioned. Unmovable. So, when Moses showed up after forty years in the wilderness and said, "Let my people go," Pharaoh didn't flinch. He scoffed. *"Who is the Lord, that I should obey him"* (Exodus 5:2)? Translation: I don't take orders from some desert God I've never heard of. I'm Pharaoh. I'm the one people bow to.

But that challenge—spoken with pride—was the beginning of a showdown that would change everything. Because God wasn't just coming for Pharaoh's title or his throne. He was coming for his heart. And when God comes for your heart, He doesn't force His way in. He corners you—patiently, powerfully, relentlessly—with grace.

The first plague came quietly but unmistakably: the Nile turned to blood. The river that gave Egypt life became a symbol of death. Pharaoh didn't budge. He called in his magicians. We can match that, he thought. So God sent frogs—millions of them. In ovens, on pillows, in bathtubs. Pharaoh started to sweat. He begged Moses to pray. Moses prayed. The frogs died. Pharaoh changed his mind.

Then came gnats. Then flies. Then the livestock died. Then boils broke out on every Egyptian. Still Pharaoh held his ground. God wasn't just sending random chaos—He was deliberately tearing down every false god Egypt trusted. Every illusion of control. Every idol of comfort and power. And Pharaoh still wouldn't surrender.

Hail. Locusts. Darkness so thick people couldn't move. Egypt was unraveling. The nation was cornered. But Pharaoh kept refusing to let go. Pride had too strong a grip. Even when the warnings grew louder, he plugged his ears. And so, the tenth plague came: the death of the firstborn.

That night, every Egyptian household wailed in grief. Including Pharaoh's. The very thing he thought he could never lose—his son, his legacy, his future—was taken. Not out of cruelty, but consequence. And in his sorrow, Pharaoh finally said the word he swore he never would: *Go.*

The Israelites were freed. But Pharaoh couldn't let it go. Even after surrendering, he sent his army to chase them down. He pursued them to the edge of the Red Sea, trying to take back the control he had just given up. And that's where the story ends—not with victory, but with a man who drowned in the wake of his own pride.

Pharaoh wasn't cornered because God hated him. He was cornered because God loved His people—and even gave Pharaoh every opportunity to turn. Every plague was a chance to let go. To lay down his crown. To be human again, instead of playing god.

But Pharaoh couldn't surrender. And when you refuse to surrender, eventually—God will let the walls close in. Not to destroy you, but to wake you up. To remind you that you are not the Author of your story. And that pretending you are will only lead to ruin. Because the truth is, God will let your plans fall apart if it means your heart can be put back together.

## What Pharaoh Teaches Us About Pride, Control, and the Cost of Refusing Surrender

The story of Pharaoh in the book of Exodus is one of the clearest biblical portraits of what happens when we refuse to let go of control—even when God gives us every opportunity to surrender.

Pharaoh ruled Egypt as a god in the eyes of the people. He had power, wealth, legacy, and pride that refused to bend. So when Moses showed up with a message from the Lord saying, "Let My people go," Pharaoh dismissed it. He didn't recognize the authority of the God of Israel. He was too confident in his own.

What followed was a divine standoff: plague after plague, each one targeting a different aspect of Egyptian strength and religious identity. Blood in the Nile, frogs, gnats, flies, disease, boils, hail, locusts, darkness—all leading up to the death of the firstborn. Each was not just a warning but an invitation: Let go. Trust God. Release control.

But Pharaoh couldn't do it. Every time he softened, he hardened again. Even after letting the Israelites go, he changed his mind and chased them into the wilderness—right into the parting waters of the Red Sea, where his pride finally drowned.

## What Can We Learn from Pharoah?

This story isn't just about a stubborn king. It's about all of us. About the parts of us that don't want to surrender, even when we can clearly see the danger of demanding control instead of yielding to God.

Pharaoh was cornered—not because God wanted to destroy him, but because God was revealing Himself. God was writing a story of rescue, and Pharaoh had a choice: join it or resist it.

In the end, this story teaches us a sobering truth: when we ignore God's voice, reject His lifelines, and cling to control at all costs, we don't just miss out on freedom—we risk being crushed by the very thing we are trying to protect. God will corner us, not to punish, but to rescue us. He'll break through pride, shake our comfort, and even disrupt our plans if it means waking us up to His better one. Surrender isn't God taking something from us—it's Him giving something far better in return: Himself.

## Balaam and the Donkey – The Story

*When you won't listen to God, don't be surprised when He speaks through a donkey, and don't miss the miracle just because it embarrasses you.*

Balaam was a prophet-for-hire. Not exactly the kind of guy you'd want leading your prayer group, but he did have a reputation for hearing from God. So when Israel showed up and started camping near Moab, the local king—Balak—panicked. He figured his army couldn't beat them, but maybe a well-timed curse could. So he sent his messengers (with a generous payment plan) to hire Balaam to pronounce a curse on Israel.

At first, Balaam said no. He actually heard from God and got clear instructions: Don't go. Don't curse Israel. They're blessed. But then the messengers came back with a better offer—more money, more honor, and Balaam suddenly needed to "check with God again." Classic move.

God allowed Balaam to go, but with a warning: Only speak what I tell you. In other words—you're not in control, Balaam.

So off Balaam went, riding his trusty donkey like he was in full prophetic command. Except . . . he wasn't. God saw that Balaam's heart was shady and his motives were off. So He sent an angel to block the road—a massive, glowing, sword-wielding angel that only the donkey could see. And here's where things get delightfully awkward.

Three times the donkey tried to avoid the angel. First, she veered off the road into a field. Balaam beat her. Then she squeezed up against a wall to dodge the angel and crushed Balaam's foot. Another beating. Finally, the donkey just laid down in the middle of the road like, "I'm not dying for this man."

That's when God opened the donkey's mouth. Yes, the donkey talked. She turned her head, looked at Balaam, and basically said, "Excuse me, have I ever acted like this before? Do I look like the kind of donkey that just throws fits for fun? Open your eyes, genius; there's something bigger going on here." And for once, Balaam was speechless. Probably more confused than he'd ever been in his life—getting life advice from a talking animal he just beat with a stick.

Then God opened Balaam's eyes, and he saw the angel standing in the road. Sword drawn. Blocking his way. It was God's way of saying, "You're not in charge here. This isn't your mission. You're not controlling the message. I am." Balaam immediately bowed low and admitted he'd sinned. But the point had been made. God used a donkey—and a blocked path—to show Balaam the truth: When your heart is set on controlling the outcome, God might just control your surroundings until you get the message.

This story isn't just funny—it's sobering. Because sometimes the road we're on seems smooth until God stops us. And if we ignore His signs, He might just let something ridiculous—or miraculous—snap us out of it.

Sometimes, it's not that we didn't hear God. It's that we didn't like what He said, so we kept riding in our own direction, hoping He'd change His mind. Spoiler: He doesn't.

## What Can We Learn from a Talking Donkey?

The story of Balaam and his talking donkey reminds us that God will go to great lengths to get our attention when our hearts are drifting off course. Balaam may have looked like he was obeying God on the outside, but inside, he was still clinging to control—trying to balance obedience with personal gain. God saw through it and used something Balaam never expected: his own donkey.

When we ignore the gentle nudges, God sometimes uses roadblocks—and occasionally even a talking animal—to stop us before we destroy ourselves. This story teaches us that obedience without surrender is just performance, and that God isn't impressed by our ability to speak if we're not willing to listen. When your path is blocked, it might not be the enemy; it might be grace in disguise.

Balaam had a donkey. Pharaoh had plagues. Me? I had four minutes of silence. No breath. No heartbeat. Just stillness. And just like them, God wasn't trying to punish me; He was trying to reach me. What happened next changed everything.

Chapter 22:

# FOUR MINUTES – THE LIE THAT DIED AND THE BREATH THAT BROUGHT ME BACK

*God didn't just give me back my breath—He gave me back my story. The lie died in those four minutes, and when I came back, I finally knew who I was: fully His, fully alive, and finally free.*

I spent half my life writing a plan I thought God would approve of—only to discover He'd already written one that was far better. I didn't need to control the story. I just needed to surrender to the Author of creation.

I didn't collapse in a church pew or fall to my knees at a revival. There were no bright lights, no angels singing. I was home—quiet, still—my Bible open in my lap as I sat beside my wife. We were doing our morning study together, something that had become a steady rhythm in this new season of surrender. After all the years I had avoided the Bible, there it was—finally open. No agenda. No guilt. No pressure to perform. Just the two of us, seeking God and simply asking Him to speak.

I wasn't just looking at the pages anymore. I was reading them and letting them read me. There was peace in that moment. The kind of peace that only comes when you stop running and finally sit still long enough to hear God whisper back.

We were talking about what we'd just read, sharing thoughts, praying over our kids, just . . . being with Him. Then it hit me—suddenly and without warning. A wave of nausea. Intense. Overwhelming. Like the whole room shifted sideways. I tried to brush it off. Shifted in my seat. Took a breath. Maybe it was nothing. Maybe I was just hungry or tired. But something in me knew that this wasn't normal.

I looked at my wife and said, "I don't feel right . . ." She turned away for just a second, and when she looked back, I was slumped in the chair. Out. Gone.

She rushed to me, called my name, shook me awake—and by God's grace, I opened my eyes just long enough for her to call the ambulance. I don't remember everything, but I remember her voice. The panic. The pace at which everything changed.

One moment, I was reading the Word I had spent a lifetime running from. The next, I was in the back of an ambulance—every breath suddenly a borrowed gift. By the time we got to the hospital, I felt better. Alert. Joking. My daughter and grandson showed up, and we were all laughing like maybe this had just been some weird false alarm.

But then it happened again. That wave of sickness. That drop. I said, "I don't feel right . . ." And just like that, I was gone. They told me later what happened: I flatlined. No breath. No pulse. No heartbeat . . . for four minutes.

And here's where the story doesn't start—it circles back. You remember the first four minutes when I was born. I told you about them in the introduction. No breath. No cry. No movement.

My mom was waiting in terror as doctors whispered diagnoses. A shadow was cast over my life before I ever had a chance to live it. That four-minute silence became the script I lived under.

But now—sitting here decades later, it was happening again. Only this time, the silence didn't define me. It freed me because this time, God didn't leave me in the silence. He rewrote it. This wasn't random. It wasn't a medical coincidence. This was God completing what He started. The same God who let me live when I didn't breathe the first time was showing me why.

Four minutes at birth. Four minutes at death. One lie buried. One life reborn. Not in a delivery room this time—but in surrender. No breath. No heartbeat. No movement:

- The same amount of time I was silent at birth.
- The same amount of time my mom held her breath waiting for me to live.
- The same length of time the doctors gave me a label, and my father weaponized it, and shame walked in like it owned the place.

This wasn't random. It was God's full circle. I wasn't in the delivery room this time; I wasn't just being born. I was being reborn. I woke up in a hospital bed, disoriented but alive. And for the first time in my life, I felt something I didn't recognize right away: freedom.

The lie was gone. The shame was silent. The weight was lifted. And I knew—those four minutes weren't just medical. They were miraculous. God took me back to the very moment the enemy first whispered, "You're not enough." And this time, He answered for me:

- "[You are] *fearfully and wonderfully made*" (Psalm 139:14).
- "You are not forsaken" (Isaiah 41:9).

- *"You are mine"* (Isaiah 43:1).
- *"If anyone is in Christ, he is a new creation"* (2 Corinthians 5:17 ESV).

I came into the world with borrowed breath, but I came back to life with grace I didn't deserve.

This is where it all ties together. The story my dad used to shame me, the silence that defined my identity, and the decades I spent walking with a Savior I wouldn't surrender to all led here:

- To a hospital bed.
- To a Bible finally opened.
- To a heartbeat I couldn't give myself.
- To a God who writes endings that feel like beginnings.

The lie died in those four minutes. I didn't.

That's the part that still takes my breath away—this time, in the best possible way. I came back with a heartbeat I didn't earn, lungs I didn't fill, and truth I couldn't have written for myself. God wasn't just saving me from death; He was saving me from the story I'd lived under.

For sixty-four years, I believed that I was broken, that I was born wrong, and hat my silence at birth was a curse I could never shake. I believed in grace for other people. I believed in calling for the qualified. But for me? I believed I was always going to be one step behind. One inch outside. One failure away from being proven unworthy. But in that second silence, something shifted.

I had always been afraid to surrender because I didn't trust what God would say once I stopped talking. But when He finally had my full attention—no heartbeat, no resistance, no noise—He didn't shame me. He didn't scold me. He breathed into me just like He did in Ezekiel 37:

*Then he said to me, "Prophesy to the breath; prophesy, son of man, and say to it, 'This is what the Sovereign Lord says: Come, breath, from the four winds and breathe into these slain, that they may live.'" So, I prophesied as he commanded me, and breath entered them; they came to life and stood up on their feet—a vast army.*

—Ezekiel 37:9–10

That's what I became. Not a mistake. Not a weak survivor. But someone who had finally been breathed into. Someone who stood not in my strength but in His. I used to think the Bible was too hard to understand, too holy for someone like me, too much truth for someone used to hiding. But when I really opened the Bible, it didn't condemn me. It called me. It named me. It reminded me of who I was before the lie: I wasn't disqualified; I wasn't defective; and I wasn't too far gone. I was a son who finally came home.

The Bible isn't a rule book; it's not a test; and it's not a flashlight to expose how bad you are. It's breath . . . It's life. It's God speaking directly into the places you've been afraid to name—telling you that your story didn't begin with silence, and it won't end with shame. It began with Him. And if you'll let Him, He'll write a better ending than the one you've believed was inevitable.

I didn't come back from the dead because of doctors. I came back because Jesus wasn't done. He wasn't done showing me the truth. He wasn't done rewriting my story. He wasn't done using my breath—not just to live, but to speak.

So, I'll say it again: The lie died in those four minutes. I didn't. And I've spent every breath since then reading the Book that saved me. It's the same Book I ran from. The same Book I feared. The same Book I left unopened for most of my life. It was never just about reading a book; it was about finally believing the One who wrote it. I don't know what lie you've been living under or what silence has shaped you. I don't know what label has been dragging behind your name since the day you were born.

But I know this: God doesn't want you to live UNREAD. He doesn't want you to settle for half-saved; He doesn't want you to carry breath in your lungs but shame in your heart. He wants you to live . . . to breathe. He wants you wants you to open His Word and finally hear the truth over every false sentence that's been spoken over you. *"Therefore, if anyone is in Christ, the new creation has come: The old has gone, the new is here"* (2 Corinthians 5:17)!

I am not the same. I've been born again—again. And this time, I came back with eyes open and a Bible I'll never close again. So, if you're still wondering what happens when you finally read the Bible, let me answer it with the only truth that matters: It will tell you who you really are. And if you let it, it might just raise the dead. I was silent for four minutes when I entered the world and silent for four minutes when I came back to life. But now that I know the truth . . . I will not stay silent anymore.

Before we turn the final page, I want to pause and say thank you. Thank you for walking this road with me—from the potholes of pain and doubt to the pages where grace finally took hold. Thank you for opening this book, even when you weren't sure where it might lead. You've made it this far, and that's not by accident. God's been in every chapter—writing, guiding, and whispering, "Keep reading."

But as much as I'm grateful for you, the final word doesn't belong to me. It never did. It belongs to God because this isn't just a story about me. It's about *the* story of the prodigal son, who wandered far but was welcomed home with open arms . . . and of the Savior who went even farther, into death itself, to make that home possible.

The prodigal son reminds us that no one is too far gone. The Resurrection reminds us that nothing is too dead to rise again. And so, when you close this book, don't think of this as an ending. See it as an invitation. A beginning. Maybe even a resurrection of your own because when God writes the story, the final chapter is always just the start of something greater.

# Chapter 23:
# RETURN AND RESURRECTION

*He runs to welcome the lost and rises to conquer death—grace that finds us and love that saves us forever.*

## The Prodigal – The Story

Jesus told the parable of the Prodigal Son in response to the Pharisees and teachers of the law grumbling that He welcomed sinners and ate with them (Luke 15:1–2). He wanted them—and everyone listening—to understand God's heart for the lost. Jesus says, *"There was a man who had two sons. The younger one said to his father, 'Father, give me my share of the estate'"* (Luke 15:11–12).

This wasn't just rude; it was like saying, "I want your money, but not you. I wish you were dead so I could get what's mine." In a patriarchal, honor-based culture, this request was scandalous. Everyone listening to Jesus's story would have expected the father to slap his son or disown him immediately.

Instead, the father shockingly divided his property between both sons, likely selling land and livestock to do it. This would have been humiliating in their village, as word spread that the father was dismantling his estate because of his rebellious son's demands.

Not long after, the younger son liquidated his assets and "*set off for a distant country*" (Luke 15:13). He was determined to leave his father, family, faith, and community behind. There, he blew through his inheritance in record time on "*wild living*"—the Greek hints at reckless indulgence, likely including parties, prostitutes, and every kind of excess.

For a while, the son probably felt invincible—everyone wanted to be his friend. But when the money ran out, his popularity disappeared, and a famine hit the land, making his situation desperate. Broke, hungry, and alone, he looked for work. The only job he could find was feeding pigs—an unclean animal in Jewish law. Jesus's audience would have been horrified at the thought of a Jewish man, knee-deep in pig slop, starving and disgraced.

He grew so hungry that he envied the pigs' pods, wishing he could fill his stomach with their food. But "*when he came to his senses*," Jesus said—like a light snapping on in the darkness—he realized even his father's hired servants had more than enough to eat (Luke 15:17). He prepared a confession he'd practiced countless times on the long road home: "*Father, I have sinned against heaven and against you. I am no longer worthy to be called your son; make me like one of your hired servants*" (Luke 15:18–19).

Notice that he didn't plan to ask for restoration as a son, just a place as a servant. Weary, filthy, and gaunt, he finally neared home. What he couldn't know was that every day, his father scanned the horizon, hoping for a familiar silhouette. Jesus says, "*But while he was still a long way off, his father saw him and was filled with compassion; he ran to his son, threw his arms around him and kissed him*" (Luke 15:20). For a dignified elder to run was undignified—his robe would have flown up, exposing his legs and shocking everyone. Yet the father didn't care. His love outweighed every cultural expectation.

The son began his speech: "*Father, I have sinned . . . ,*" but the father didn't let him finish. He called his servants: "*Quick! Bring the best robe and put it on him. Put a ring on his finger and sandals on his feet*" (Luke 15:22). The robe covered his rags; the ring restored his status as son; sandals meant freedom (slaves went barefoot). Then the father ordered: "*Bring the fattened calf and kill it. Let's have a feast and celebrate. For this son of mine was dead and is alive again; he was lost and is found*" (Luke 15:23–24). The entire household erupted with music, dancing, laughter, and joy.

Meanwhile, the older brother—who had stayed and worked dutifully in the fields—heard the music as he came near the house. He asked a servant what was happening. The servant answered: "*Your brother has come, and your father has killed the fattened calf because he has him back safe and sound*" (Luke 15:27).

The older brother's face must have hardened. Instead of joy, he burned with resentment. He refused to go inside. His father came out—again humbling himself—and pleaded with him. But the older son exploded:

> *Look! All these years I've been slaving for you. . . . Yet you never gave me even a young goat so I could celebrate with my friends. But when this son of yours, who squandered your property with prostitutes, comes home, you kill the fattened calf for him!*
>
> —Luke 15:29–30

Notice the contempt: "*this son of yours,*" not "my brother." He saw himself as a servant slaving away, not as a beloved son. The father's reply was filled with tenderness: "*My son, . . . you are always with me, and everything I have is yours. But we had to celebrate . . . because this brother of yours was dead and is alive again; he was lost and is found*" (Luke 15:31–32).

Jesus ended the parable there, leaving the ending unresolved: Would the older brother enter the celebration, or remain outside in bitter pride?

## What Can We Learn from the Prodigal Son?

The story of the prodigal son isn't just a parable—it's a mirror that reflects our rebellion, our pride, our wandering hearts, and the radical love of a father who never stops watching the road for our return. In this story, Jesus paints a picture of two sons—one who runs far and fast, chasing a life he thought would satisfy, and another who stays home, checking every box but missing his father's heart. Both are lost in different ways. Both misunderstand grace. And both are invited into something better.

The younger son reaches his breaking point in a pigsty—filthy, ashamed, rehearsing his apology. He expects rejection. He gets a robe. He expects a lecture. He gets a feast. The father doesn't just forgive; He runs toward his son. He doesn't just allow the son back—He restores him fully. This is the gospel: that while we are still a long way off, God sees us, moves toward us, and covers our shame with His love.

But the story doesn't end with the celebration. It zooms out to show us the older brother—offended, bitter, unwilling to come in. His obedience had become currency. His pride had become a prison. He wasn't physically far from his father, but his heart was miles away.

This parable cuts through both illusions—the illusion of self-made goodness and the illusion that we're too far gone. It reminds us that transformation doesn't begin with trying harder or cleaning ourselves up: It begins with coming home. The Father wants us back, not as servants, but as sons and daughters. He doesn't wait with arms crossed; He runs with arms wide open.

This story is the gospel in miniature: grace for the guilty, compassion for the broken, and a celebration that neither son could have earned. It's a reminder that God's plan has always been restoration—not just of behavior, but of identity. And it points to the cross, where the cost of our rebellion was paid in full by Jesus so that we could be welcomed home with no strings attached.

Whether you've run far away or stayed close but hardened your heart, the invitation is the same: Come inside. Drop the act. Join the feast. Because grace isn't just available—it's running down the road to meet you.

## When Death Lost Its Grip – The Story

*The cross shows how far God would go to save us; the empty tomb proves He did.*

In the quiet shadows of Gethsemane, Jesus prayed with anguish deeper than words. He knew what awaited Him: betrayal, torture, a brutal death. His sweat fell like drops of blood as He cried, *"Father, if you are willing, take this cup from me; yet not my will, but yours be done"* (Luke 22:42).

His closest friends, whom He asked to watch and pray, slept nearby, unaware of the spiritual battle unfolding. Suddenly, torches lit the darkness as Judas arrived, leading a mob of soldiers and officials. He greeted Jesus with a kiss—a sign of love turned into a symbol of treachery. Jesus, calm and resolute, stepped forward: *"Do what you came for, friend"* (Matthew 26:50).

Peter tried to defend Jesus, drawing a sword and cutting off the ear of Malchus, the high priest's servant, but Jesus rebuked him: *"Put your sword back in its place. . . . Do you think I cannot call on my Father, and he will at once put at my disposal more than twelve legions of angels"* (Matthew 26:52–53)? Yet He chose the path of surrender, the path of love.

The disciples fled into the night, terrified. Jesus was bound and led away to a mock trial before the Sanhedrin, where false witnesses twisted His words. Through it all, He remained silent like the prophecy foretold: *"He was oppressed and afflicted, yet he did not open his mouth; he was led like a lamb to the slaughter"* (Isaiah 53:7).

When the high priest demanded, *"Are you the Messiah, the Son of the Blessed One?"* Jesus replied with unwavering authority: *"I am . . . and you will see the Son of Man sitting at the right hand of the Mighty One and coming on the clouds of heaven"* (Mark 14:61–62). The leaders tore their robes, declaring Him worthy of death.

At dawn, they brought Jesus to Pilate, the Roman governor. Pilate questioned Him, found no guilt, yet feared the raging crowd. To appease them, he offered a choice: Release Jesus or Barabbas, a violent rebel. The crowd, stirred by the priests, shouted, *"Crucify him"* (Mark 15:13)! Pilate washed his hands before them: *"I am innocent of this man's blood"* (Matthew 27:24), but he condemned Jesus to death.

Roman soldiers stripped Jesus, flogged Him until His back was torn open, and mocked Him with a crown of thorns pressed into His scalp. They spat on Him, struck Him, and knelt in cruel parody: *"Hail, king of the Jews"* (Matthew 27:29)! They forced Him to carry His cross through the crowded streets of Jerusalem, but as His strength failed, a man named Simon of Cyrene was seized to carry it.

They led Him to Golgotha—*"the place of the skull"*—and nailed Him to the cross between two criminals. The sky grew dark at noon, as though all creation mourned. Jesus looked at those who mocked and tortured Him and prayed the unthinkable: *"Father, forgive them, for they do not know what they are doing"* (Luke 23:34).

From the cross, He spoke words of love and completion. To the thief who asked to be remembered, He promised: *"Truly I tell you, today you will be with me in paradise"* (Luke 23:43). He entrusted His mother Mary and the disciple John into each other's care. Then He cried out, *"My God, my God, why have you forsaken me?"* (Mark 15:34), fulfilling Psalm 22 and expressing the agony of bearing the world's sin.

Finally, with His last breath, He declared: *"It is finished"* (John 19:30), and *"Father, into your hands I commit my spirit"* (Luke 23:46). At that moment, the temple curtain tore from top to bottom— God's powerful sign that the barrier between humanity and Himself was forever removed. The earth shook, rocks split, tombs broke open, and a Roman centurion gasped, *"Surely he was the Son of God"* (Matthew 27:54)!

Jesus's body was taken down by Joseph of Arimathea, wrapped in linen, and laid in a new tomb sealed with a heavy stone. Guards were posted to prevent rumors of His resurrection. Darkness and silence settled, and all hope seemed lost.

But early on the first day of the week, as dawn broke, Mary Magdalene and other women went to the tomb to anoint Jesus's body. They found the stone rolled away and the tomb empty. Angels appeared, shining with glory, and said: *"Why do you look for the living among the dead? He is not here; he has risen"* (Luke 24:5–6)!

Mary Magdalene ran to tell the disciples, breathless with wonder. Peter and John raced to the tomb, finding only the grave clothes folded. That evening, Jesus appeared to His disciples behind locked doors, saying, *"Peace be with you"* (John 20:19)!

He showed them His hands and side, proving He was alive— not a ghost, but risen in glorified flesh. Over forty days, He appeared to more than five hundred people, teaching, restoring, and commissioning His followers. One morning on a mountain in Galilee, Jesus gathered His disciples and gave them the Great Commission: *"Go and make disciples of all nations . . . teaching them to obey everything I have commanded you. And surely, I am with you always, to the very end of the age"* (Matthew 28:19–20).

Then, on the Mount of Olives, He blessed them, and as they watched, He ascended into heaven. He is seated at the right hand of the Father, reigning forever as King of kings and Lord of lords (Acts 1:9–11).

## What Can We Learn from Jesus's Death and Resurrection?

The death and resurrection of Jesus Christ aren't just the climax of the Bible—they are the foundation of our hope, the heartbeat of the gospel, and the clearest picture we have of God's love.

Through the cross, we see a God who didn't stay distant, but stepped into our pain, our guilt, and our shame—willingly. He didn't die because we were good. He died because He is good. The cross screams, "You are worth dying for." And the empty tomb declares, "Nothing—not sin, not shame, not even death—can stop My love."

In Jesus's final breath, every ounce of humanity's sin was laid on His shoulders. And in His first breath after rising, every chain of death was broken. The resurrection isn't just proof of life after death—it is proof that God keeps every promise. That grace is real. That forgiveness is possible. That we're not too far gone. And that when Jesus says, "*It is finished,*" He means it.

What can we learn from this story? That salvation is a gift, not a reward. We don't earn it, we receive it. The gospel doesn't begin with "behave"; it begins with "believe." It invites every soul—broken, bitter, burned-out, or brand new—to come home. Just like the prodigal son, we're not met with judgment, but joy. We're not handed a list of demands; we're wrapped in love and welcomed into the family.

This story is still changing lives today because people are still drowning in guilt, still running from grace, still wondering if there's any hope left. And the answer remains the same: Jesus is alive. That means you can be too, not just one day in heaven—but right now. A new life. A new identity. A new beginning.

If you've never accepted Jesus as your Lord and Savior, or maybe you have but you've wandered and want to come home, don't let this moment pass you by. You don't have to fix yourself first. Just come as you are. He's not waiting with crossed arms—He's waiting with open arms. The Bible says, *"Everyone who calls on the name of the Lord will be saved"* (Romans 10:13).

If you're ready, here's a simple prayer. You don't need perfect words. Just an honest heart:

> Lord Jesus, I know I'm a sinner and I need Your grace. I believe You died for me and rose again so I could live. I give You my heart, my past, and my future. Forgive me. Save me. Be my Lord and Savior. From this moment on, I'm Yours. In Jesus's name, Amen.

If you prayed that, welcome home.

If you just accepted Jesus as your Savior or if you've rededicated your life to Him, your next step is to find a Bible-believing church. Look for one that teaches Jesus as the only way to salvation, preaches the truth of God's Word, and walks in grace, not guilt. You weren't meant to walk this journey alone. Find a community that will help you grow, encourage your faith, and remind you that you're part of God's family now.

So now what?

That's what the next (and final) chapter is all about. I want to give you a few simple tools that helped me finally open God's Word and keep reading it. You don't have to use them all. Just take what helps. What happened in those four minutes changed my life, but what I did after—opening the Bible—changed everything.

# Chapter 24:

# HOW TO READ THE BIBLE (AND NOT FALL ASLEEP OR RUN SCREAMING)

*True teaching is not just passing on knowledge, but inviting others to see the beauty of God's truth—because every lesson learned in His Word shapes a life to look more like His.*

I didn't write this lesson from scratch or come up with these tips out of thin air. I researched, learned from others, and compiled what I found most helpful. Some of it, I've used myself, and some I haven't tried yet. My goal in including it here is simple: to offer you practical tools that might make reading God's Word a little less intimidating, a lot more rewarding, and maybe even fun. Think of this chapter as a buffet—take what helps you, leave what doesn't, and come back for seconds when you're hungry for more.

Have you ever tried reading the Bible and felt like you needed a decoder ring or a seminary degree just to figure out who's who and what's what? Welcome to the club. You're not alone, but you don't need a doctorate in theology to hear God speak. Reading Scripture isn't about impressing scholars or collecting gold stars; it's about connecting with the God who loves you and wants you to know Him.

So, here's a collection of real-world, real-person strategies to start reading—and loving—your Bible like someone who wants a relationship, not just religion. It's not magic, but it can make a world of difference on your journey.

And hey, if nothing else, at least you'll know where to find the verses proving that mosquitoes were on the ark. (Spoiler: They were, unfortunately.)

## Start Where It Makes Sense

The Bible isn't a single book; it's a library—a sixty-six-book collection of poetry, history, prophecy, letters, and more. And let's be real: you wouldn't walk into a library, grab a dictionary off the shelf, and expect it to read like a thriller. In the same way, diving straight into Leviticus as your first Bible read is like trying to start a new fitness routine by entering a CrossFit competition. It'll leave you confused, sore, and wondering what just happened.

So, where should you start? Head straight for the Gospels: Matthew, Mark, Luke, or John. They're like the front-row seat to Jesus's life and teachings. Want action? Mark is Jesus's highlight reel—fast-paced, packed with miracles, and perfect if your attention span is shorter than your coffee order. Prefer something deeper? John is like a late-night conversation with Jesus where He tells you why He came and what He wants for your life.

**Pro Tip:** Start small. A chapter a day is better than trying (and failing) to read an entire book in one sitting. The goal isn't speed—it's understanding.

## Choose a Translation You Understand

Your translation could be the difference between aha! and huh? If your Bible sounds like, "Verily, thou knowest not what thou readest," it might be time for an upgrade. Consider these options.

| Bible Version | Best For | Why It Works |
|---|---|---|
| NLT (New Living Translation) | New believers and devotion | Sounds natural—like Jesus is talking to you over coffee. |
| NIV (New International Version) | Suitable for new and mature believers | Super readable, but faithful to original meaning. |
| CSB (Christian Standard Bible) | Study + good blend of accuracy and readability | Clear, modern; great for understanding. |
| ESV (English Standard Version) | Deep study | More formal; closer to original grammar. |
| MSG (The Message) | Emotional punch | Paraphrase; great to use alongside another Bible version. |

## Always Read with Prayer

The Bible isn't a textbook; it's a conversation with God. Take at least thirty seconds before you start to pray: "Lord, open my eyes. Teach me through Your Word." James 1:5 says if we lack wisdom, we should ask, and God loves giving it.

## Read for Relationship, Not Religion

You don't build a friendship by memorizing someone's LinkedIn profile—or by quoting random one-liners they've said. Yet so many of us approach the Bible that way. The Bible isn't a list of motivational quotes; it's the story of God's relentless love. Read like you're spending time with Someone who loves you.

## Understand Context

Context is king. Without it, you risk turning profound truth into comic nonsense. Example: Philippians 4:13 isn't about CrossFit. It's about contentment in suffering.

**Three context questions to ask:**
1. Who wrote the Scripture passage?
2. Who were they writing to?
3. What's happening before and after the portion of Scripture you're reading?

Context doesn't water down Scripture—it brings it to life.

## Recognize the Different Types of Literature

The Bible includes these genres:

- **Poetry** (e.g., Psalms): "*The Lord is my shepherd*" is a metaphor.
- **Law** (e.g., Leviticus): Cultural guidelines for Israel.
- **Prophecy** (e.g., Isaiah): Calls to repentance and foretelling.
- **Narrative** (e.g., Genesis, Acts): Real-life stories showing God at work.
- **Epistles** (e.g., Romans): Teaching letters for churches.
- **Wisdom** (e.g., Proverbs): Timeless principles, not promises.
- **Apocalyptic** (e.g., Revelation): Symbolic visions of God's victory.

Each genre invites a different reading lens.

## Additional Strategies to Help You Start Reading and Loving Your Bible

- **Learn to Interpret Responsibly:** Avoid reading your ideas into Scripture (eisegesis). Aim to draw God's truth out (exegesis). Seek authorial intent. That is, seek to understand what the biblical author, inspired by God, originally meant before trying to apply the Scripture to your life.

- **Beware the "Verse of the Day" Trap:** A verse-a-day app is a nice supplement, but real growth comes from reading whole chapters.

- **Take Notes and Journal:** Capture what stands out. Record questions. Reflect. Write honestly. It helps the Word sink deeper.

- **Memorize Verses:** They're spiritual fuel. Start with a few selected verses:
    - ›› John 14:6
    - ›› Romans 8:28
    - ›› Philippians 4:6

  Use repetition, visuals, sticky notes, or music. Make it fun.

- **Don't Study Alone:** God designed faith to flourish in community. Join a group. Ask questions together. Text a friend about what you read.

- **Learn the Bible's Big Story:** From Genesis to Revelation, it's one story—Jesus is the thread. Look for connections:
    - ›› Abraham's sacrifice → Jesus
    - ›› Passover lamb → Jesus
    - ›› Jonah → Jesus's burial and resurrection

- **Handle Difficult Passages with Humility:** Some verses are hard. That's okay. Ask questions. Use tools. Don't twist them; let God teach you through them.

- **Approach Hard Truths with an Open Heart:** If the Bible never challenges you, you might not be listening. Let it shape you.
- **Make Bible Reading Part of Your Life, Not a Chore:** Read during breakfast. Listen during your commute. Fit it into your natural rhythm. It's a relationship, not a checklist.
- **Let Scripture Read You:** Hebrews 4:12 says Scripture is alive. Ask not just, "What does a passage mean?" but "What does it reveal about me?"
- **Remember You're Not the Hero:** Jesus is the hero of the Bible—and your life. Let that truth bring peace, not pressure.
- **Celebrate Progress:** A verse read while holding a crying baby counts. God honors your steps, however small.
- **Don't Compare Your Journey:** This is your walk with Jesus. Not Instagram's.
- **End Every Reading with Prayer:** Talk to God about what you read. Ask Him to help you live it out.

## Final Thoughts: Keep Going

These aren't rules; they're invitations—tools to help you meet with the Author Himself. Open His Word again tomorrow. And again after that. He's waiting—and He speaks.

www.ingramcontent.com/pod-product-compliance
Lightning Source LLC
Chambersburg PA
CBHW060021100426
42740CB00010B/1551